COLD ★ WAR MASSACHUSETTS

JOSHUA SHANLEY

THE History PRESS

Published by The History Press
An imprint of Arcadia Publishing
Charleston, SC
www.historypress.com

First published 2025

Manufactured in the United States

ISBN 9781467157896

Library of Congress Control Number: 2025931117

For Robert Joseph Comerford, PhD.

CONTENTS

ACKNOWLEDGEMENTS

This book would not have been possible without the unwavering support and love of my wife, Kristen. Her patience, encouragement and belief in my work provided the foundation for this project. I am deeply grateful to all the people at the Massachusetts Emergency Management Agency (MEMA), especially director Dawn Brantley, deputy director Patrick Carnevale and Rich Latour, assistant director of operations, for their support throughout this project. Their insights and assistance were instrumental in bringing this book to life. A special thank you to Lieutenant Colonel Geoffrey Love, director of historical services for the Massachusetts National Guard. His dedication to preserving and sharing history has been a great source of inspiration. I also extend my gratitude to Mark Foster, Massachusetts Task Force 1 (retired), for sharing his incredible wealth of knowledge and resources collected over a storied career. His contributions significantly enriched the content of this book. Mike Kinsella, your assistance with helping me negotiate this process has been invaluable. Sean Colby at FalloutFiveZero.com, your incredible knowledge of this material and your willingness to share it with me were instrumental. Thank you for your generosity and passion for history. Finally, I want to express my appreciation to the hundreds of local historical societies, libraries and museums whose resources I used during the writing of this book. The staff and volunteers of these institutions generously shared content that made this book more rich and detailed. Your dedication to preserving our history is truly commendable.

Thank you all for your contributions and support. This book is as much yours as it is mine.

INTRODUCTION

The Cold War era significantly impacted Massachusetts, transforming the state into a strategic hub of military and civil defense activities. Massachusetts was home to numerous military bases where missiles were stored and maintained. These installations played a crucial role in national defense, with radar systems set up to detect potential threats. The state also became a center for advanced communications, essential for maintaining coordination during a crisis.

Civil defense in Massachusetts involved coordinated efforts at federal, state and local levels. Federal initiatives were complemented by state programs, ensuring comprehensive preparedness across all regions. Local governments, particularly in Boston and other cities, developed their own civil defense strategies. Public and private shelters were established to protect the population in case of an attack, and regular drills were conducted to ensure readiness. Warning systems were put in place to provide early alerts in the event of an emergency.

Research institutions in Massachusetts, such as MIT and Lincoln Labs, contributed significantly to advancements in technology during the Cold War. Their work in fields like radar, energy and medical research supported national defense efforts. These institutions also pioneered innovations that improved radar capabilities, crucial for detecting and responding to threats.

Overall, the Cold War period saw Massachusetts evolve into a critical component of the United States' defense infrastructure, with extensive military installations, robust civil defense mechanisms and cutting-edge research facilities.

PART I

★

CIVIL DEFENSE AND MILITARY PREPAREDNESS

MASSACHUSETTS'S ROLE IN COLD WAR CIVIL DEFENSE

Early Beginnings and the Historical Context

Committees on Public Safety

The origins of civil defense and emergency management in Massachusetts can be traced back to the American Revolution, at which time ahead of impending war, citizens banded together to prepare—not just for battle, but with a wider perspective that was inclusive and comprehensive. Three separate but connected Committees on Public Safety were established first in anticipation of the Revolution in 1774, again for America's entry into World War I in 1917, and for a third time in 1940 as fighting in Europe and the Pacific escalated.

First Committee on Public Safety (1775–1776)

John Hancock was the chairman of the first Committee on Public Safety, established in 1774 and charged "to keep careful watch on any person attempting the destruction, invasion, detriment or annoyance of the provinces." Clearly in anticipation of the impending Revolution, the nine members of the committee organized the storage of provisions, tools, weapons and munitions at Worcester and Concord. Additionally, the committee established a network of watchmen and couriers who pledged to deliver vital information at a moment's notice. The system was activated on April 18, 1775, when committee member Paul Revere began his famous ride.

Second Committee on Public Safety (1917–1918)

On February 14, 1917, as tensions concerning the United States' abilities to avoid being drawn into World War I in Europe increased, Massachusetts Governor Samuel McCall established the Committee on Public Safety, a powerful group made up of one hundred members from across the commonwealth tasked with coordinating a comprehensive list of agencies and resources, including military, industry and economic sectors. A bulletin distributed from the Committee on Public Safety in August 1917 described that it was established "in order that Massachusetts be ready in the event of any National emergency, to co-operate with the Federal and State officials to the fullest extent of her resources." An article in the *Boston Globe* noted that comments from Governor McCall highlighted that "the extent of the unpreparedness was greater than anybody appreciated, and urged active work along many lines war or no war, crisis or no crisis." The committee, chaired by Boston lawyer and investment banker James J. Storrow and funded with over $2 million appropriated by the state legislature, recommended a permanent bureau be established made up of three divisions. The first would be to inventory and analyze the textile industry in Massachusetts, which might be used to produce uniforms and tents. The second division would catalogue other factories and machine shops capable of producing weapons and munitions. The third division listed skilled labor sectors. By November 1917, 245 cities and towns across Massachusetts had established local committees on public safety and donated $100,000 to support the broader initiatives of the Commonwealth.

The Committee on Public Safety was indeed comprehensive in its approach. Subcommittees included Finance and Service Bureau ("in charge of coordinating the efforts of patriotic and preparedness organizations"), the latter of which also was assigned to coordinate volunteer groups. The Medical and Sanitary committee organized activities of hospitals and the American Red Cross, and the Bureau of Industrial Survey coordinated activities of textiles, engineers, materials and food. There was a separate Railroad Transportation subcommittee and another on Military Affairs to coordinate equipment and recruiting. The Committee on Public Safety was again dissolved in 1918, nine days after the armistice that ended World War I.

Civil Defense Measures During World War II

Third Committee on Public Safety

The third iteration of the Committee on Public Safety was established by Governor Leverett Saltonstall on August 23, 1940. He appointed 150 citizens to direct what would ultimately become a "homefront force of civilian volunteers…made available for a wide range of non-protective activities essential to our total wartime program"; 438,000 men and women from around Massachusetts served during the four years.

In November 1940, an extensive survey for bomb shelters took place in Boston, led by well-known local architects in cooperation with the army, the city Planning Board and the National Resources Board. The efforts focused on locating all strong structures to which Boston citizens could resort in case of an attack. This survey was part of a "civilian public safety program" undertaken by the American Institute of Architects. The first section studied was Charlestown, particularly the area around the Navy Yard, identified as the principal strategic point for an enemy's attack on Greater Boston. Volunteer workers from the Harvard School of Architecture were involved in this project. The list of shelter locations was to be furnished to city authorities, and similar studies were underway in other major cities of New England. Subways were ruled out as shelters due to the risk of gas attacks and the potential interference with transportation.

By September 1941, 319 of the 351 cities and towns in the commonwealth had a functional local program running, with the remaining 32 partially ready. While a central mission of these civil defense groups was organized around air raids, there soon developed a more broad preparedness initiative as well, including medical support, communications, transportation and more. By 1942, civil defense units were integrated with established public safety departments in planning, training and exercises and ultimately during actual incidents. When a spate of ships was sunk off Cape Cod during the summer of 1942, local teams proved their mettle and received national recognition. Elsewhere in Massachusetts, other civilian defense units were assisting at plane crashes and worked directly with police and fire departments. Attack on the East Coast continued to become a growing concern as the war waged on in Europe, and Civilian Defense units filled more roles in staffing warning systems until the end of the war in 1945, when, on June 30, the Committee on Public Safety was once again dissolved.

Civil Defense Act of 1950

On October 9, 1949, Massachusetts Representative John F. Kennedy expressed his concerns about the inadequate progress in the federal civil defense planning program in a letter to President Truman. He highlighted the urgency of preventing what he termed an "Atomic Pearl Harbor," criticizing the General Services Administration for having only one individual working full time on civil defense planning, a role recently assigned by the National Security Resources Board.

President Harry S Truman initially viewed civil defense as a state and local responsibility. However, the Soviet Union's first atomic test in 1949 and the outbreak of the Korean War in 1950 prompted a shift. Truman established the Federal Civil Defense Administration (FCDA) in December 1949 to organize and coordinate national civil defense efforts, followed by the Federal Civil Defense Act of 1950, which provided the FCDA with statutory authority to plan, guide and assist state and local civil defense efforts. Additionally, the administration promoted industrial dispersal to minimize the impact of potential attacks.

In response to federal initiatives, Governor Paul Dever issued a series of executive orders to align Massachusetts with national civil defense strategies throughout 1950. Executive Orders No. 1 through No. 19, enacted throughout the year, established local civil defense organizations, appointed directors, organized regions and set up various emergency services such as medical, police and fire services specifically for civil defense purposes (US CD before 1950). However, by June 1950, many Massachusetts municipalities had not participated fully in the process. The Massachusetts Civil Defense Agency (MCDA) was formally established on July 20, 1950, with John F. Stoker, state commissioner of public safety, appointed as director.

In a significant move, on August 12, 1950, the U.S. government released information on the effects of atomic bomb attacks, lifting previous security restrictions. John W.M. Bunker, dean of the Graduate School at MIT and a technical advisor to the Massachusetts Civil Defense Agency, stated that survivors of an atomic attack need not fear lingering radioactivity if proper precautions are taken. This announcement aimed to educate the public on radiological facts, highlighting the importance of informed civil defense. Massachusetts conducted its first major test alert at Revere Beach in the summer of 1950, involving a mock atomic bomb attack by an enemy submarine. This exercise brought together various civil defense and armed forces units, including the National Guard, Coast Guard Auxiliary and

On September 12, 1952, Governor Dever enacted Executive Order No. 17, regulating travel of uniformed and civilian Federal Armed Forces personnel during civil defense alerts. *Massachusetts Emergency Management Archives (MEMA).*

Civil Air Patrol. The demonstration aimed to test the coordination between civilian defense and armed forces in a beach defense scenario.

Still, in September 1950, 156 out of Massachusetts's 351 cities and towns had failed to meet Governor Dever's deadline for appointing local civil defense directors, as mandated in his executive order.

On December 6, 1950, the governor revealed that metropolitan Boston was identified as the seventh most likely target for an enemy atomic attack in the country, based on federal assessments. This disclosure further emphasized the necessity of a robust civil defense infrastructure. The governor's office had been actively working on reactivating the State Guard, ensuring it could be organized quickly in response to any threats. A $10,000 appropriation for civil defense was included in the pending supplemental budget. On December 17, the Massachusetts Civil Defense Agency, under the direction of John F. Stokes, announced the state's air raid signal system. The two-stage public warning code included a "red alert" for imminent attacks and an "all clear" signal for when it was safe. This system was part of the broader effort to ensure the state was adequately prepared for potential enemy attacks.

The state's civil defense efforts were extensive and well coordinated. The Massachusetts Civil Defense Agency had split the state into nine regions, with over thirty-five communities already establishing their local defense organizations. These regions were prepared to reactivate World War II–era

The 1952 Boston Civil Defense Manual outlines the city's strategies for integrating community and industry resources into comprehensive civil defense plans. *Boston Public Library.*

organizations and were developing local ordinances and bylaws to align with the new state civil defense act. This involved creating an inventory of materials, facilities and services available for emergency use.

Springfield was particularly proactive. Following the onset of the Korean War, local police and civil defense agencies swiftly mobilized. Police officers were put on extended shifts, and air raid warden training was intensified. A combined emergency effort involving various local organizations, including the Boy Scouts and the FBI, demonstrated the city's commitment to preparedness. This collaboration aimed to ensure all vital points and utilities were protected and that a quick response system was in place.

Furthermore, Springfield officials engaged in state-level discussions about civil defense measures. They worked on a draft ordinance based on Chapter 639 of the Acts of 1950, intending to use it as a model for other communities across Massachusetts. The ordinance was designed to integrate local and state efforts, ensuring a cohesive and comprehensive approach to civil defense.

By February 1951, Governor Dever had signed a special appropriation bill, allotting $180,500 to the State Civil Defense Agency. This funding covered administrative assistants and office personnel who would assist mayors and city managers serving as regional directors. Additionally, Attorney General Francis E. Kelly ruled that loyalty oaths must be taken by all individuals connected with civil defense activities to prevent potential saboteurs from undermining the program.

In the summer of 1951, hospitals in Massachusetts received instructions to prepare for atomic emergencies. They were advised to discharge a significant portion of their patients to make room for casualties and to stockpile blood and plasma. The state civil defense agency's plan also called for hospitals to manufacture their intravenous fluids to ensure sufficient medical supplies during a crisis.

President Dwight D. Eisenhower continued the philosophy that civil defense was primarily a state and local responsibility, with the federal government providing guidance and support. His administration emphasized evacuation plans over building a nationwide shelter system. The FCDA was merged with the Office of Defense Mobilization to form the Office of Civil and Defense Mobilization, aiming to improve organizational efficiency.

During this period, Governor Christian A. Herter enacted a series of executive orders addressing both immediate disaster response and long-term preparedness planning. For instance, Executive Order No. 20 addressed emergency housing for victims of a tornado on June 9, 1953.

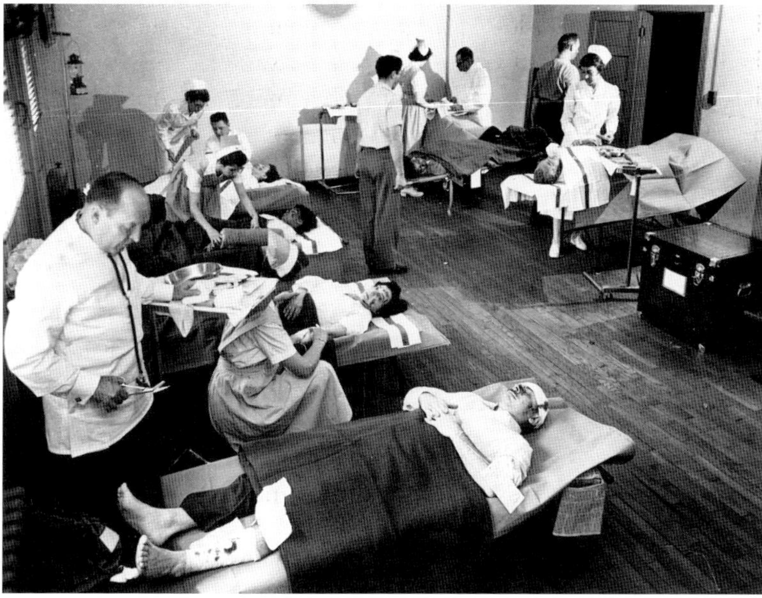

Personnel demonstrate a two-hundred-bed portable hospital at Eastern States Exposition, West Springfield. Developed by the FCDA, it fits in a single van for rapid deployment. *Digital Commonwealth.*

Governor Christian A. Herter of Massachusetts (*left*) discusses a model air raid shelter with A.D. O'Connor, regional administrator of the FCDA, in West Springfield, 1953. *Digital Commonwealth.*

Above: Governor Volpe and state civil defense director Maginnis post Massachusetts's first fallout shelter sign at the Statehouse on November 5, 1962. *National Archives*.

Opposite, top: Daniel J. Finn, state director of civil defense (1963–65), uses a portable radio in front of the mobile disaster control center vehicle, coordinating response efforts. *MEMA*.

Opposite, bottom: A Massachusetts State Police sergeant stands outside the Civil Defense Communications Center in Framingham, preparing for Hurricane Edna's impact in 1954. *Digital Commonwealth*.

MASSACHUSETTS
MOBILE DISASTER CONTROL CENTER
S1133
MASSACHUSETTS
MOBILE DISASTER CONTROL CENTER
MOTOROLA

OPERATIONS
MASSACHUSETTS
STATE POLICE

Orders No. 22 and No. 23 responded to specific weather emergencies, and broader civil defense initiatives were reflected in Orders No. 25 and No. 26, which focused on civil defense planning by state agencies and the reorganization of the state civil defense structure, respectively.

In March 1954, Colonel John J. Maginnis, the Massachusetts Civil Defense director, addressed the public about the improbability of evacuating Boston in the event of a sudden atomic attack. He emphasized that, without sufficient warning time, citizens would be safer taking cover rather than attempting to evacuate. Maginnis highlighted ongoing efforts to develop a warning system for timely evacuations and urged participation in civil defense exercises to better prepare for potential attacks.

Toward the later 1950s, MCDA began to incorporate initiatives more broad than atomic attack to include natural disasters, in large part major flooding following hurricanes and tornado in Massachusetts that required significant response and recovery efforts. Governor Foster Furcolo's executive orders between 1957 and 1961 focused on enhancing the state's civil defense and emergency response capabilities.

1960s

By the early 1960s, the Massachusetts Civil Defense Agency was charged with coordinating emergency functions for military and natural disasters across the state. However, only a third of cities and towns had adequate civil defense agencies, with another third having marginal units and the rest having none. This gap in preparedness was partly due to a lack of organization and partly due to the misconception among local officials that their role was only significant in the event of a major bomb drop. Civil defense focused on medical self-help training courses through the U.S. Public Health Service to address the shortage of doctors and nurses during disasters. Additionally, programs were initiated to train laymen in caring for injured family members, providing water and food safety and ensuring proper nursing care.

By 1961, the state was grappling with the evolving nature of nuclear threats and the need to balance state and local control over defense strategies. Maginnis recognized these challenges and stressed the importance of statewide coordination while also supporting local initiatives. Comprehensive planning for shelters, evacuation procedures and fallout responses became increasingly essential as the nuclear threat grew more sophisticated.

In the early 1960s, both the Federal and Massachusetts Civil Defense Agencies operated from the same headquarters at 143 Speen Street, Natick. *MEMA*.

In 1961, a hypothetical scenario involving atomic bombs was simulated in Western Massachusetts as part of Operation Alert—1961. Civil defense forces conducted this exercise, which estimated that 249,000 residents would have died and another 85,000 would have been injured if real bombs had exploded near Memorial Bridge and Longmeadow. The exercise assumed a thick layer of radioactivity over Greater Springfield, effectively leveling the city's skyline. The bombs were theorized to be of ten-megaton strength, equating to ten million tons of TNT.

The Massachusetts Hospital Association, in cooperation with the Department of Health, Education and Welfare and the Civil Defense Agency, launched a training program at Fort Devens to teach hospital personnel how to operate emergency hospitals. This program was the first of its kind in the United States. The agency's efforts were recognized as a crucial step in preparing for potential disasters, with the Massachusetts Civil Defense Agency playing a significant role in organizing and conducting these programs.

The Cuban Missile Crisis in 1962 significantly heightened the state's alert status. During this period, Maginnis was actively involved in assessing the state's preparedness alongside Governor Volpe and other key advisors. They discussed the need for additional funding and resources to strengthen civil defense measures. Maginnis's presence in Washington, where he received briefings from high-level national security officials, underscored the critical nature of the situation. These briefings highlighted the urgency of enhancing civil defense efforts in light of the imminent threat.

Governor Volpe took proactive steps to bolster the state's civil defense infrastructure. He urged families to build fallout shelters and accelerated the program to establish protective shelters in public and private buildings. The governor communicated the severe nature of the crisis to local officials, emphasizing the need for immediate action. At that time, only a small fraction of potentially suitable buildings had been licensed for federal stockpiling of supplies, highlighting the urgency of the situation. Additionally, plans for emergency evacuation routes were expedited, although it was acknowledged that in the event of a direct nuclear strike, evacuation would be impractical and sheltering in place would be necessary.

Maginnis's role in these efforts reflects several key aspects of his leadership in civil defense. Public education was a priority, as he understood the necessity of raising awareness about the realities of nuclear war and the actions needed to mitigate its impact. Balancing the complexities of state-level coordination with local implementation of defense strategies was another critical aspect of his work. The Cuban Missile Crisis, in particular, showcased his skills in crisis management and highlighted the vital importance of civil defense during a period of potential national emergency. Maginnis's involvement in high-level discussions and planning efforts demonstrated the seriousness with which the state government approached the threat of nuclear war.

President John F. Kennedy significantly increased civil defense funding, focusing on the construction and stocking of fallout shelters. His administration's initiatives included a comprehensive survey of existing shelters and programs to build new ones in deficit areas. Governor John A. Volpe's executive orders during this period reflected these federal initiatives, focusing on civil defense structure and personnel management and ensuring robust emergency preparedness and public safety measures were in place.

Between 1963 and 1965, federal initiatives under Presidents Kennedy and Lyndon B. Johnson influenced Governor Endicott Peabody's executive orders. Efforts to enhance civil defense capabilities and public safety infrastructure were evident in orders to reorganize and enhance the state's civil defense structures. Several federal initiatives under Presidents Johnson and Kennedy influenced Governor Volpe's second term. Executive orders

In May 1961, President Kennedy met with governors, including Massachusetts Governor Volpe, to discuss civil defense amid growing international tension and shelter-building efforts. *JFK Library.*

Built in the 1960s, this concrete bunker in Westborough was once the regional headquarters of the MCDA. It is now operated by the Massachusetts Environmental Police. *Photo by the author.*

This bunker in Bridgewater was the Region 2 headquarters for the Massachusetts Civil Defense Agency, providing a command center for emergency operations and disaster response. *Photo by the author.*

focused on enhancing the state's emergency preparedness infrastructure and communications systems, aligning with federal guidelines and ensuring comprehensive preparedness and response capabilities.

The Massachusetts Civil Defense Agency continued to expand its infrastructure. In addition to opening the new underground headquarters in Framingham in 1963, during the latter 1960s, regional offices were opened at hardened facilities in the Belchertown State School, on the grounds of the Tewksbury and Bridgewater state hospitals and in a concrete bunker in Westborough.

1970s and Beyond

During the Nixon, Ford and Carter administrations, federal civil defense policies continued to evolve, influencing state-level actions. Key initiatives included Nixon's review of the national shelter system, Ford's crisis relocation planning and Carter's integration of the Defense Civil

Preparedness Agency into FEMA. All had minimal effects on civil defense initiatives in Massachusetts.

At the state level, in the mid-1970s, the Massachusetts Civil Defense Agency faced significant changes and challenges. Governor Michael S. Dukakis, aiming to trim the state's budget, announced cuts to the agency in February 1975. These cuts were part of broader cost-reduction efforts and included a 75 percent reduction in the civil defense budget, which involved consolidating fourteen area offices into four or five and maintaining only a small central office and a training facility in Framingham. The agency's director, Louis Saba, indicated that such reductions were part of widespread governmental retrenchment.

Despite these cutbacks, the Massachusetts Civil Service Commission ordered the rehiring of thirty laid-off civil defense employees in November 1975. The budget cuts, incorporating reductions from the previous administration under Governor Francis W. Sargent, left the Civil Defense Agency with only forty-three employees and no room for expansion beyond the present strength, despite the federal government covering half of the agency's expenditures.

The state's civil defense program was under scrutiny for its preparedness. By September and March of the previous year, surveys revealed that about 280 of the state's 351 communities had inadequate civil defense programs. Many cities and towns had incomplete emergency plans and deteriorating equipment, with some supplies like food and medicine being destroyed or removed from shelters.

During this period, the agency prepared for potential nuclear threats. Robert Cunningham, who replaced Louis Saba as the director of the Civil Defense Agency in late 1975, outlined plans developed with federal funds to relocate residents from high-risk areas like metropolitan Boston and parts of Cape Cod in case of a nuclear attack. This relocation plan was aimed at minimizing exposure to fallout and ensuring public safety.

The general public's indifference toward civil defense was highlighted by the dilapidated state of shelters and inadequate emergency plans. Saba pointed out that funding for civil defense had been halved over the past decade, reducing the agency's staff from 112 to 39 people. Local civil defense efforts, once robust, had declined, with communities treating these programs as nonessential due to tight budgets.

By early 1976, the state's budget, reflecting Dukakis's cuts, allocated $305,000 to the Civil Defense Agency, significantly less than previous years. This constrained budget hindered the agency's ability to expand or improve

Plaque dedicated to Robert J. Boulay, featuring a photo with Governor Dukakis, mounted outside the State Emergency Operations Center. Boulay served from 1955 to 1990. *MEMA*.

its preparedness measures. Despite the challenges, the agency continued to focus on public safety, including plans for radiation monitoring and emergency communication.

One notable event did occur in 1974, when a bomb threat in Boston led to significant federal investigation and panic. A letter sent to Boston Police Commissioner Robert diGrazia demanded $200,000 to prevent the detonation of a bomb. The letter also claimed that a nuclear device would be triggered if the demands were not met. This threat instigated an extensive investigation by both local and federal authorities.

A copy of the letter was sent to the FBI, which sparked a high-level investigation involving various federal agencies. The threats were taken seriously due to the specifics mentioned in the letter and the use of complex language that hinted at a scientific background. The bomb threat occurred during a period of heightened sensitivity, given the ongoing Watergate scandal and other national security concerns.

The nuclear component of the threat greatly alarmed authorities, as it implied not just a large-scale explosion but also potential radioactive fallout, which would have devastating long-term effects. At the time, the idea of nuclear terrorism was a new and terrifying concept, amplifying the fear and urgency surrounding the threat. The mention of a nuclear bomb necessitated a full-scale investigation involving multiple federal agencies, including the FBI and the Atomic Energy Commission.

Despite the extensive investigation, no evidence of a nuclear bomb was found. The threat was eventually deemed a sophisticated hoax.

Details of the bomb threat and the nuclear aspect of the hoax were not made fully public at the time. The authorities handled the situation with a high level of confidentiality to avoid widespread panic. Public knowledge was limited, and the full scope of the investigation, including the seriousness with which the threat was taken, was not disclosed to the general public until years later. The secrecy was likely a strategic decision to prevent causing alarm among the citizens and revealing vulnerabilities in national security protocols. It wasn't until investigative reports and retrospectives like the one published in the *Boston Sunday Globe* in 1981 that the public learned about the extent and nature of the threat and the subsequent federal response.

In the early 1980s, the Reagan administration revitalized civil defense with a more aggressive posture toward the Soviet Union, leading to renewed public focus on the potential for nuclear war. This period also saw the Three Mile Island Nuclear Station accident in March 1979. Following the 1986 Chernobyl disaster, emergency planning zones were developed around Massachusetts. These events collectively spurred the revitalization of civil defense initiatives throughout the decade.

In the early 1980s, Massachusetts developed a comprehensive evacuation plan known as "Hubbub" to prepare for potential nuclear war threats. This plan aimed to relocate nearly 500,000 vehicles from metropolitan Boston, directing residents of Cambridge to Greenfield, Somerville to Maine and

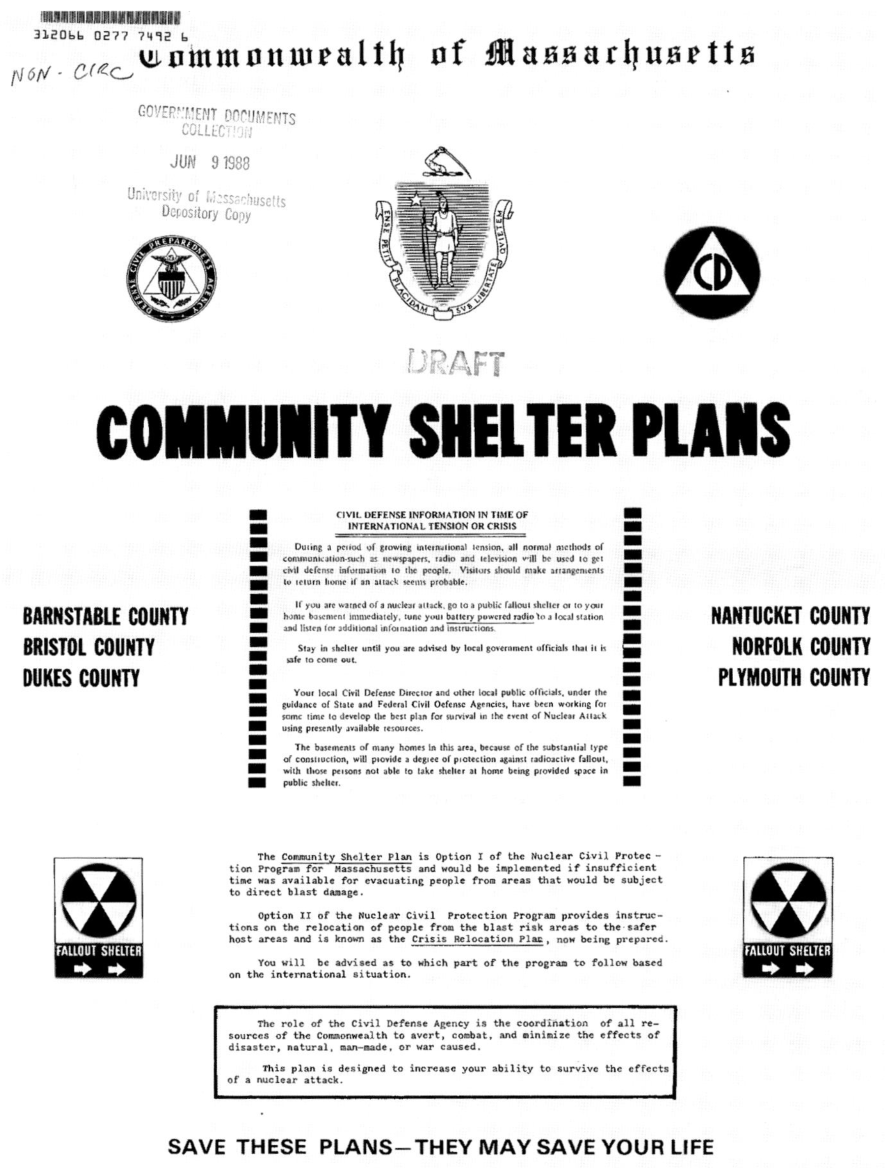

Commonwealth of Massachusetts

DRAFT

COMMUNITY SHELTER PLANS

BARNSTABLE COUNTY
BRISTOL COUNTY
DUKES COUNTY

CIVIL DEFENSE INFORMATION IN TIME OF INTERNATIONAL TENSION OR CRISIS

During a period of growing international tension, all normal methods of communication-such as newspapers, radio and television will be used to get civil defense information to the people. Visitors should make arrangements to return home if an attack seems probable.

If you are warned of a nuclear attack, go to a public fallout shelter or to your home basement immediately, tune your battery powered radio to a local station and listen for additional information and instructions.

Stay in shelter until you are advised by local government officials that it is safe to come out.

Your local Civil Defense Director and other local public officials, under the guidance of State and Federal Civil Oefense Agencies, have been working for some time to develop the best plan for survival in the event of Nuclear Attack using presently available resources.

The basements of many homes in this area, because of the substantial type of construction, will provide a degree of protection against radioactive fallout, with those persons not able to take shelter at home being provided space in public shelter.

NANTUCKET COUNTY
NORFOLK COUNTY
PLYMOUTH COUNTY

FALLOUT SHELTER

The Community Shelter Plan is Option I of the Nuclear Civil Protection Program for Massachusetts and would be implemented if insufficient time was available for evacuating people from areas that would be subject to direct blast damage.

Option II of the Nuclear Civil Protection Program provides instructions on the relocation of people from the blast risk areas to the safer host areas and is known as the Crisis Relocation Plan, now being prepared.

You will be advised as to which part of the program to follow based on the international situation.

FALLOUT SHELTER

The role of the Civil Defense Agency is the coordination of all resources of the Commonwealth to avert, combat, and minimize the effects of disaster, natural, man-made, or war caused.

This plan is designed to increase your ability to survive the effects of a nuclear attack.

SAVE THESE PLANS—THEY MAY SAVE YOUR LIFE

In the 1970s, Massachusetts developed plans for each county to evacuate or shelter communities in response to a nuclear attack, ensuring civil defense readiness. *UMass Amherst Libraries.*

Quincy to Cape Cod. The plan required families from various Greater Boston communities to move to safer locations in Western Massachusetts, Cape Cod, Maine or New Hampshire. The governor and his top staff would monitor the evacuation from an underground bunker in Framingham, overseeing the relocation of approximately 4.3 million Massachusetts residents, including 2.1 million from the Boston area. This strategic evacuation was not a fanciful notion but a carefully devised plan by the state's Civil Defense Agency to handle a mass exodus in the event of a nuclear threat.

By 1981, MCDA had refined the plan to detail evacuation routes and procedures for 202 communities in the state, especially those near strategic military bases, high-population areas or key industries. Additionally, about 400,000 Connecticut residents and 150,000 Rhode Island residents would be directed to Massachusetts, with 2 million more from neighboring states passing through on their way to northern New England. This would result in Massachusetts experiencing significant movement, more than any other state, as noted by the Civil Defense Agency.

Further demonstrating the state's commitment to civil defense, in 1984, officials highlighted the feasibility of evacuating residents near the Seabrook, New Hampshire nuclear power plant in case of a serious accident. This plan involved cooperation between federal and state agencies, requiring an emergency declaration by the governors of Massachusetts and New Hampshire. The Seabrook Radiological Emergency Response Plan, finalized after two years of preparation, outlined procedures for evacuating over seventy-five thousand residents within a ten-mile radius of the plant. Public hearings were scheduled to finalize this comprehensive emergency response plan, reflecting input from local authorities and addressing their needs.

The Massachusetts Civil Defense Agency, under the leadership of Robert J. Boulay, coordinated this plan. The agency, along with the Massachusetts National Guard, Department of Public Health, State Police and Massachusetts Bay Transit Authority (MBTA), would implement the evacuation, with the MBTA providing over one hundred buses to transport residents to designated reception centers where the Red Cross would offer food and shelter. Secure sirens and the Emergency Broadcast System would notify residents of an emergency.

In the aftermath of the Chernobyl nuclear accident in 1986, the Massachusetts Civil Defense Agency sought further expertise to enhance its emergency preparedness. Governor Michael Dukakis enlisted Albert Carnesale, a Harvard professor and nuclear weapons control expert, to assess

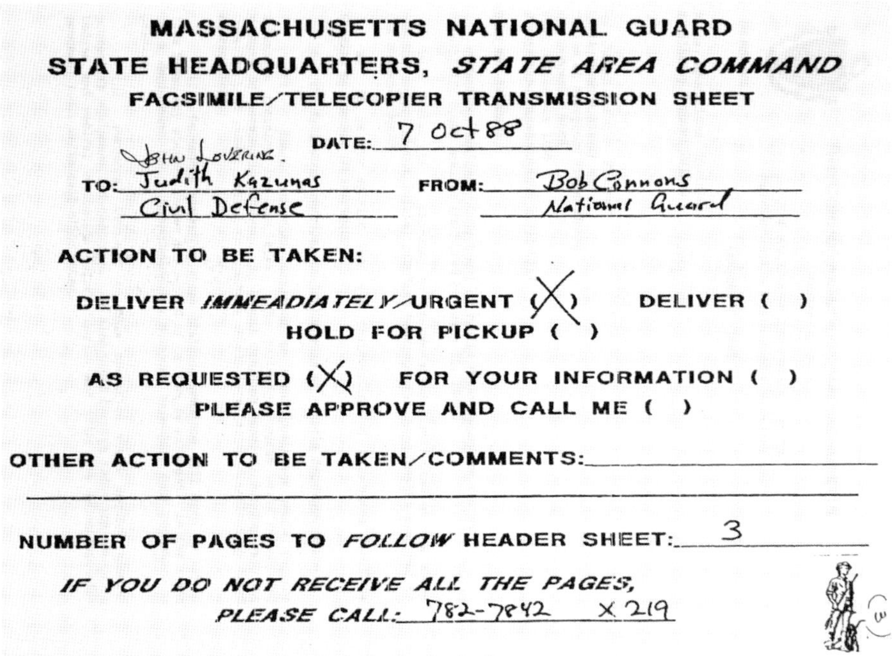

MASSACHUSETTS NATIONAL GUARD
STATE HEADQUARTERS, *STATE AREA COMMAND*
FACSIMILE/TELECOPIER TRANSMISSION SHEET

DATE: 7 Oct 88

TO: John Lovering. Judith Kazunas, Civil Defense

FROM: Bob Connors, National Guard

ACTION TO BE TAKEN:

DELIVER *IMMEADIATELY*/URGENT (X) DELIVER ( )
HOLD FOR PICKUP ( )

AS REQUESTED (X) FOR YOUR INFORMATION ( )
PLEASE APPROVE AND CALL ME ( )

OTHER ACTION TO BE TAKEN/COMMENTS:

NUMBER OF PAGES TO *FOLLOW* HEADER SHEET: 3

IF YOU DO NOT RECEIVE ALL THE PAGES,
PLEASE CALL: 782-7842 X 219

This 1988 fax cover sheet was used during an MCDA nuclear evacuation drill for processing evacuees in case of an accident at the Pilgrim Nuclear Power Station, Plymouth. *UMass Amherst Libraries*.

the implications of the Chernobyl disaster for the Seabrook evacuation plans. Carnesale's role included examining the distribution of radioactive debris, its intensity and the appropriate size of the evacuation zone. He aimed to identify improvements in evacuation procedures and reduce the likelihood of an accident. His involvement emphasized the importance of learning from the Chernobyl incident to enhance local safety measures.

THE COLD WAR DILEMMA

DEFENSE AND MILITARY ASSETS

Evacuation versus Sheltering: Strategies and Challenges

During the early Cold War, U.S. civil defense strategies focused on sheltering and evacuation to protect people from nuclear attacks. These approaches had different implications and evolved due to advancements in nuclear weapons technology and political changes.

Early Sheltering Efforts

The notion of building public shelters in Boston predates the Cold War. In late 1940, before the United States entered World War II and in the midst of the London Blitz, Boston conducted a detailed survey to identify potential bomb shelter locations. Prominent local architects led this initiative in collaboration with the army, the city Planning Board and the National Resources Board. Their goal was to pinpoint sturdy structures that could serve as shelters during an attack. These locations were compiled into a list and provided to city authorities. Similar efforts were carried out in other major cities in New England. The first area of focus was Charlestown, particularly around the Navy Yard, which was considered a key strategic point for potential enemy attacks on Greater Boston. The Harvard School of Architecture worked on this survey as part of a broader "civilian public safety program" by the American Institute of Architects.

The main targets for bomb shelters included the basements of steel-constructed buildings and the central floors of steel or concrete buildings that were eight stories or taller. Additionally, the survey considered underground spaces that could be easily adapted. However, subways were not considered for shelters due to the dangers posed by gas attacks and the risks associated with electrified third rails and interference with transportation.

The Storrow estate in Lincoln, Massachusetts, currently part of the Carroll School, features a bomb shelter constructed in 1940. Recognized as New England's first bomb shelter, it was built on the property owned by banker and philanthropists James and Helen Storrow. The timing of its construction, a year before the United States entered World War II, when the threat to the U.S. mainland was minimal, has prompted curiosity. The shelter is notably large, with rooms reinforced by thick concrete walls, intended to house people for extended periods and to store supplies and furniture. Despite speculation, the Storrows claimed that the structure was not a bomb shelter but was meant for storing apples.

FEDERAL CIVIL DEFENSE ADMINISTRATION INITIATIVES

Initially, the FCDA emphasized blast-resistant shelters to protect from immediate nuclear explosion effects like blast waves and radiation. Financial and logistical challenges, however, made it difficult to implement a comprehensive shelter program. Congress was reluctant to fund large-scale shelter construction, seeing it as endorsing communistic living and state centrism.

By the mid-1950s, the FCDA had shifted to mass evacuation, planning to relocate urban populations to rural areas during a nuclear threat. Suburban and farm families were expected to house and feed city evacuees. This plan faced skepticism, as many suburbanites were unwilling to host evacuees, and the logistics of such mass movement were doubtful, especially with multi-megaton hydrogen bombs.

Hydrogen bombs made evacuation plans less viable due to widespread fallout. The FCDA's strategy assumed people could quickly move out of targeted areas and that rural areas would be safe from fallout. This assumption proved unrealistic since fallout could spread over large areas, complicating safety measures.

Given evacuation limitations, the focus returned to sheltering, particularly fallout shelters designed to protect against radioactive fallout. These shelters were practical and could be integrated into existing buildings at a lower cost. The Office of Civil Defense (OCD) promoted dual-purpose shelters that could serve as community centers or other public facilities in peacetime and as fallout shelters during an attack.

Public and political opinion on civil defense measures fluctuated. There was significant support for fallout shelters, but political and economic considerations hampered implementation. The debate centered on whether the federal government should fund and manage a national shelter program. Critics argued that extensive civil defense preparations could make nuclear war seem more winnable, while proponents viewed it as a necessary precaution.

Civil Defense Programs in Boston

During the early 1950s, Boston implemented a comprehensive civil defense program to enhance its preparedness and response capabilities in the face of potential emergencies. The city's schools were integral to this effort. Both public and parochial schools designated shelter areas and conducted monthly air raid drills. Civil defense materials were widely distributed, and first aid training became a mandatory course for students in grades seven through twelve. The involvement of Home and School Associations ensured that school buildings could be efficiently utilized as temporary shelters during emergencies.

Boston also focused heavily on communications and practical exercises. A series of tests and exercises was conducted to develop and assess the civil defense organization. For instance, a major communications test in August 1951 involved various methods, including telephones, police radios and amateur radios. Following this, the city held its first citywide test to evaluate siren coverage and traffic control. By May 1952, these exercises had expanded to include participation from the entire metropolitan area. Additionally, Boston took part in a Command Post Exercise under the Federal Civil Defense Region I to enhance communication capabilities between cities and states in the Northeast.

The city's air raid warning and shelter programs were equally comprehensive. A total of 119 sirens were installed across Boston to provide

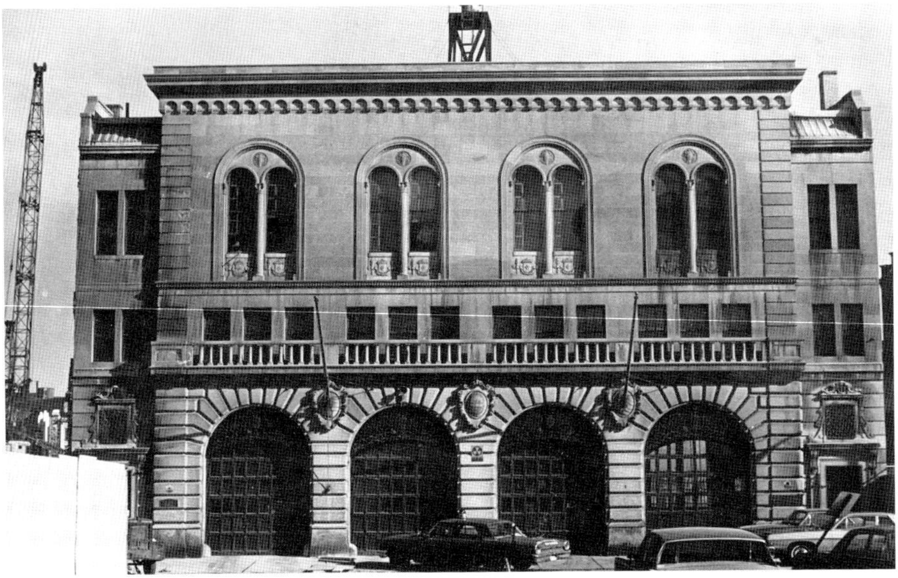

In Boston, fire stations like this served as fallout shelters with air raid sirens on their roofs to alert residents of potential attacks. *City of Boston Archives.*

early warnings. Reinforced steel frame buildings and subway stations were surveyed and designated as public shelters, with the Traffic Department taking responsibility for posting and maintaining shelter signs. Detailed surveys and procedures ensured these shelters were suitable and accessible.

Medical and health services were another critical component of Boston's civil defense strategy. The Medical Health Division organized emergency medical services, forming first aid teams and training thousands of first aiders. Schools and university buildings were designated as improvised hospitals, and blood bank assistants received specialized training. Health service teams were also established to handle environmental sanitation during emergencies.

The Social Services Division played a vital role in coordinating efforts between public and private welfare services. This division provided shelter, clothing, food, financial aid and rehabilitation services. Volunteers from schools, churches, labor organizations and businesses were mobilized, and comprehensive training programs were implemented to ensure readiness.

Boston's Building Department conducted a thorough survey of all reinforced steel frame buildings over five stories high. They approved 301 buildings for use as public shelters and collaborated with building owners to ensure their availability. The Traffic Department took on the responsibility of

Massachusetts civil defense notice from around 1960, detailing air raid signals. Citizens were urged to learn "alert" and "take cover" signals to ensure preparedness. *City of Boston Archives.*

posting and maintaining shelter signs. Additionally, 29 subway stations were evaluated, and 27 were designated as shelters. The Building Department issued instructions on how to locate and safely access these shelter areas. This comprehensive survey process included using mine detectors to verify the steel framed construction of buildings when necessary.

The civil defense guidelines also recommended that households prepare their own shelters. Ideal locations included basements or interior corridors of large buildings. These areas were advised to have minimal glass, multiple exits, proper ventilation and emergency supplies such as food, water and first aid kits. Recommendations included reinforcing ceilings and ensuring the availability of battery-operated lighting and emergency communication tools.

Public and Private Sector Involvement

Boston's business and industrial sectors were actively involved in civil defense efforts. Banks, hotels, retail stores and industrial plants developed detailed plans, selected shelter areas, trained personnel and conducted regular drills. These sectors maintained close coordination with civil defense officials to ensure an integrated response.

The city's transportation and public utilities were also part of the civil defense framework. Detailed plans managed the city's transportation needs during a disaster, with specific assembly areas designated for commercial vehicles. Continuous communication was maintained through advanced radio systems. Public utilities participated in all test exercises and contributed significantly to the distribution of civil defense literature.

Public information and education were crucial for ensuring widespread awareness and participation. The Public Information Division utilized

The "Alert America" Convoy in Copley Square, used to promote civil defense following Boston's first postwar air raid alert, emphasizing citizens' responsibilities during the Cold War era. *Digital Commonwealth.*

newspapers, radio, television, public displays and other media to disseminate civil defense information. Efforts included mass mailings, public exhibitions and educational programs designed to engage the public and promote preparedness.

Ground Observer Corps and Operation Lookout

The Ground Observer Corps (GOC) played a crucial part in the defense strategy of Massachusetts during the Cold War. Its creation was prompted by the limitations of radar technology in detecting low-flying aircraft. Executive Order No. 9, issued in 1951 by Governor Paul A. Dever, officially established the GOC in Massachusetts. The order placed the organization under the control of the adjutant general of the commonwealth, who was responsible for establishing observation posts across the state. These posts, strategically placed about eight miles apart, were to be manned by civilian volunteers. The primary responsibility of the GOC was to supplement the air force's radar system by visually identifying and reporting low-flying aircraft.

Operation Lookout, a simulated air raid exercise, took place from September 10 to 18, 1949. This operation, the first of its kind since World War II, encompassed ten northeastern states. During Operation Lookout, over 2,200 volunteers manned 245 observation posts throughout Massachusetts. These posts were integrated with a network of coastal radar stations to test the efficacy of their combined operation. One notable instance during the operation involved a simulated attack by more than one hundred National Guard planes. An alarm originating from a secret air defense control center in New York City was transmitted to Radio Station WNBC in Port Washington, New York. From there, the alarm was relayed to Station WBZ in Boston and to a key air raid warning center in Montpelier, Vermont.

The GOC was later transferred from the adjutant general to the Massachusetts Civil Defense Agency in 1955. This shift, enacted through Executive Order No. 28 by Governor Christian A. Herter, was deemed necessary to optimize military and civil defense efforts. Under the new order, cities and towns with observation posts were directed to cooperate with both the director of civil defense and the U.S. Air Force in establishing and running these posts. While the provided documents don't offer details on an Operation Sky Watch, they do highlight the vital contributions of women in various civil defense roles, including the GOC. Women's roles ranged from administrative and clerical work to more specialized tasks such as radio operators, telephone operators and administrative officers within the GOC. They were crucial in ensuring smooth communication and administrative efficiency within the organization.

Challenges and Changes in Civil Defense

In June 1950, the *Boston Globe* reported on the discovery of a private bomb shelter on Brimmer Street in Boston's Back Bay neighborhood, which was inadvertently revealed due to an explosion. The shelter had been built without permits and was unknown to public officials, including the police commissioner and the building commissioner. The shelter had been constructed by Judge F. Delano Putnam, an army veteran and former judge appointed by Governor Foster Furcolo as a special justice of the Boston Municipal Court in 1930. This one-way structure, reinforced with steel and concrete, featured two doors made of Brimmex steel, each weighing about three hundred pounds. Despite the secrecy surrounding its construction, the shelter did not conform to civil defense standards, as the walls inside were not reinforced.

In December 1950, a meeting took place between Massachusetts Governor Paul A. Dever and President Truman regarding a proposed multifunctional facility in Boston that would serve as both a garage and a bomb shelter. The Reconstruction Finance Corporation had authorized a $12 million loan for the project, which required a $3 million collateral from the company. Mayor John Hynes of Boston emphasized the urgency of the project for alleviating parking issues and providing a protective measure against potential aerial attacks during the Cold War era. This dual-purpose facility was seen as a vital development to enhance both the city's infrastructure and its preparedness for possible threats.

The same month, the *Boston Globe* introduced the "Civil Defense Forum," a new service designed to guide New Englanders on their involvement in civil defense organizations. The forum highlighted the roles of various community members, from nurses to policemen in Massachusetts, in the event of a bomb disaster. It addressed specific inquiries from local residents, such as a fisherman from Marblehead seeking to contribute to harbor defense and an individual from Quincy with a cabin cruiser ready to assist, pointing them toward local civil defense initiatives and the Coast Guard Auxiliary. In 1951, the forum profiled the Franklin Park Zoo in Boston, which had designated the cellar of the zoo's birdhouse as a bomb shelter for its elephants.

In 1951, the Massachusetts Bay Transportation Authority (MBTA) announced a bomb shelter would be built under Beacon Hill, integrated into a new $11,500,000 subway link. This stretch of the subway, between Park Street and Scollay Square, was part of the oldest street railway subway in the United States. The MBTA planned to increase the thickness of the concrete over the two-rail tube to provide additional protection. Along the "spine" of the subway, extra shelter spaces would be created to accommodate more people during emergencies. The platform at Park Street was to be widened, further enhancing its capacity to serve as a bomb shelter. Additionally, first aid rooms would be incorporated into the design to address medical needs during and after an attack. At its deepest point, the shelter would have forty feet of solid soil overhead, offering unparalleled protection compared to any other section of the subway system.

In the event of an air raid warning, the public was instructed to move to designated shelters or the nearest subway or deep basement. If these were

In 1951, under Governor Paul Dever, the MCDA pamphlet requested Massachusetts building owners and occupants utilize existing facilities for optimal shelter availability. *Massachusetts Statehouse Library*.

not accessible within three or four minutes, people were advised to find cover behind walls, in ditches or in ravines to protect against flying debris and heat effects. After the initial blast, it was crucial to stay under cover for a few minutes to avoid falling debris. The procedures emphasized calmness to prevent panic and detailed steps for administering first aid and managing small fires.

Community Involvement and Public Sentiment

Boston's business and industrial sectors were actively involved in civil defense efforts. Banks, hotels, retail stores and industrial plants developed detailed plans, selected shelter areas, trained personnel and conducted regular drills. These sectors maintained close coordination with civil defense officials to ensure an integrated response.

The city's transportation and public utilities were also part of the civil defense framework. Detailed plans managed the city's transportation needs during a disaster, with specific assembly areas designated for commercial vehicles. Continuous communication was maintained through advanced radio systems. Public utilities participated in all test exercises and contributed significantly to the distribution of civil defense literature.

Public information and education were crucial for ensuring widespread awareness and participation. The Public Information Division utilized newspapers, radio, television, public displays and other media to disseminate civil defense information. Efforts included mass mailings, public exhibitions and educational programs designed to engage the public and promote preparedness.

In December 1960, the *Boston Globe* reported on the notable progress made by Civil Defense (CD) organizations in suburban communities despite widespread public indifference. These organizations were dedicated to enhancing public safety and preparedness, largely driven by unpaid directors who led small volunteer groups. They faced significant challenges, particularly public apathy, as they were often referred to as "crackpots" due to the relentless focus on defense preparation.

Various examples illustrated the proactive measures taken by these directors to improve civil defense readiness. In towns like Scituate and Arlington, initiatives were launched to establish bomb shelters and increase the capacity of existing CD units. These efforts proved practical during emergencies, such as a hurricane in Scituate, where the CD's assistance was invaluable.

In 1963, Boy Scouts in Gardner helped stockpile supplies and water containers in the licensed public shelter at the U.S. Post Office, aiding local preparedness efforts. *MCDA*.

In 1963, the Massachusetts Civil Defense Training School in Topsfield hosted a two-week rescue course, attended by New England departments and rated best in the nation by the Department of Defense. *MCDA*.

Training grounds for civil defense played an important role, alongside the federal government's provision of matching funds to local communities for constructing and remodeling local centers. This financial support was crucial in bolstering local preparedness efforts.

Additionally, evacuation plans for towns and the distribution of radiological monitoring kits to high schools reflected a comprehensive strategy to prepare for potential atomic bomb threats. These measures underscored the extensive efforts made to ensure community readiness in the face of potential disasters.

In 1960, a proposal was made to construct a massive nuclear bomb shelter beneath Boston Common. This shelter was intended to protect people from atomic radiation, marking it as the first of its kind in the United States. Integrated with a new underground garage, the shelter was feasible due to the water discovered during the garage's excavation. The proposed facility was to cover six acres and include three levels, capable of converting from a parking structure to a shelter swiftly. Its design featured

FCDA regional administrator A.D. O'Connor and two Boston regional office personnel inspect Geiger counters, circa 1960, ensuring their readiness for radiation detection tasks. *Digital Commonwealth.*

an exceptionally strong arched roof, fifteen times more resilient than a flat top, to shield against radiation and debris. Provisions for food, clothing, medical supplies and dormitory spaces were planned to sustain twenty-two thousand people for up to two weeks. The shelter also included independent systems for electricity, water, ventilation and sewage treatment. The project had an estimated cost of $71 million, with $34 million allocated for the garage alone. The Massachusetts Parking Authority, responsible for the project, anticipated its completion by July 1961. This proposal was part of a broader civil defense strategy, reflecting the heightened concern for public safety during the Cold War era. Approval from local officials was required, highlighting the community's role in addressing the nuclear threat.

Continued Efforts and Public Response

By 1960, CD initiatives in suburban communities demonstrated both progress and notable reluctance. Efforts led by CD directors, many of whom were unpaid, showed significant advancement despite public apathy. These directors worked diligently to enhance local preparedness, obtaining better communication equipment and more detailed plans. This progress was largely attributed to the persistent efforts of dedicated volunteers and a few paid directors in communities like Marshfield, Arlington and Peabody.

Significant progress included the establishment of facilities such as bomb shelters and hospitals. For example, Norwell maintained a two-hundred-bed hospital for emergencies, while Arlington reported constructing one of the first apartment-type shelters in the nation. Similarly, Scituate was recognized for its tireless work during Hurricane Donna, utilizing the town's generator when power was lost.

Despite these advancements, reluctance toward CD initiatives was prevalent among suburban residents. A primary factor was the fear of reduced property values if home bomb shelters were added. This concern

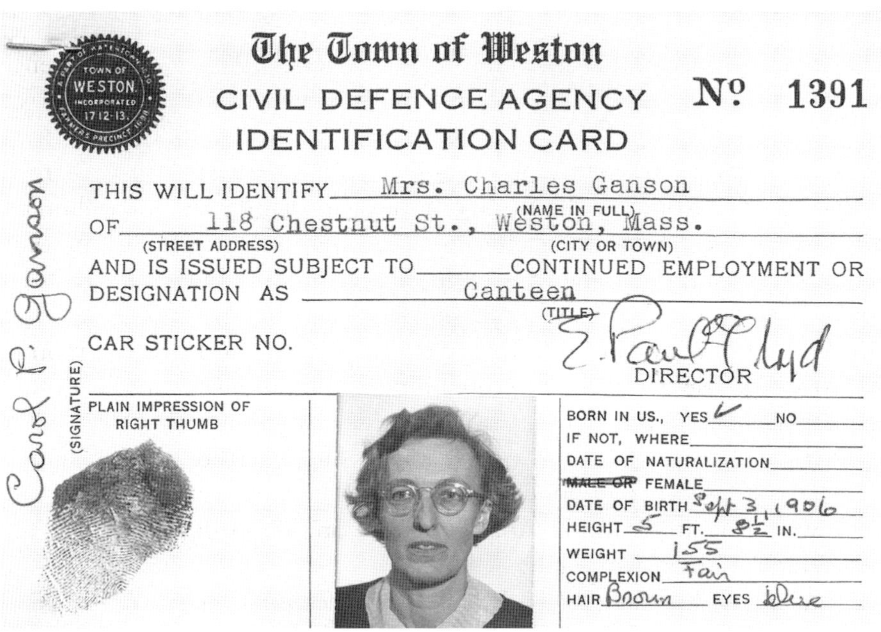

The Town of Weston

CIVIL DEFENCE AGENCY №. 1391

IDENTIFICATION CARD

THIS WILL IDENTIFY Mrs. Charles Ganson
(NAME IN FULL)

OF 118 Chestnut St., Weston, Mass.
(STREET ADDRESS) (CITY OR TOWN)

AND IS ISSUED SUBJECT TO ___ CONTINUED EMPLOYMENT OR DESIGNATION AS Canteen
(TITLE)

CAR STICKER NO.

E. Paul O'Lloyd
DIRECTOR

(SIGNATURE) Carol F. Ganson

PLAIN IMPRESSION OF RIGHT THUMB

BORN IN US., YES ✓ NO
IF NOT, WHERE
DATE OF NATURALIZATION
~~MALE OR~~ FEMALE
DATE OF BIRTH Sept 3, 1906
HEIGHT 5 FT. 8½ IN.
WEIGHT 155
COMPLEXION Fair
HAIR Brown EYES blue

This example from Weston shows a civil defense volunteer ID card, common for providing personal information, a photo and assignment designation for emergency roles. *Weston Historical Society.*

was compounded by the fear of ridicule from neighbors, discouraging many from constructing such shelters. Additionally, a bill proposed to exempt civil defense shelters from increased real estate taxes failed to pass, further disincentivizing homeowners.

Some communities assessed no additional taxes for building shelters, provided they were used strictly for that purpose. However, only a few families in towns like Concord and Lexington built such shelters, indicating widespread hesitation. In places like Arlington, geographical limitations, such as low land preventing the construction of underground shelters, also hindered efforts.

In October 1960, a year before the Cuban Missile Crisis, JFK warned the nation to "maintain the best attainable protection for the civilian population against the major effects of a thermonuclear attack." In Massachusetts, this call to action was largely heeded, but at the state level, the debate over building shelters or planning for evacuation of population centers continued.

State-Level Debates and Federal Surveys

The matter remained undecided at the state level. At a press conference in Boston on August 9, 1961, Governor Volpe was asked if he preferred completing the national highway program or constructing blast-proof bomb shelters, each costing about $40 billion. As expected from a road builder, Volpe favored the highway program, noting that the $40 billion for roads would be spread over sixteen years, whereas bomb shelter funding would need immediate allocation. He argued that highway expenditures could be a future investment, potentially boosting the economy, while bomb shelters would be useless in a direct hit. Yet the following month, the governor addressed the improbability of a mass evacuation in Boston in the event of a nuclear attack, suggesting that only rural areas of Maine, New Hampshire and Vermont might have enough time for such an action. In southern New England, especially in Massachusetts's large cities, there would be an almost complete reliance on fallout shelters due to the congested urban environment.

Governor Volpe shared insights from his recent meetings with officials from the Central Intelligence Agency and Civil Defense in Washington, revealing that individuals in bombed areas would have only about forty-five minutes to reach safety. He emphasized the practicality of private fallout

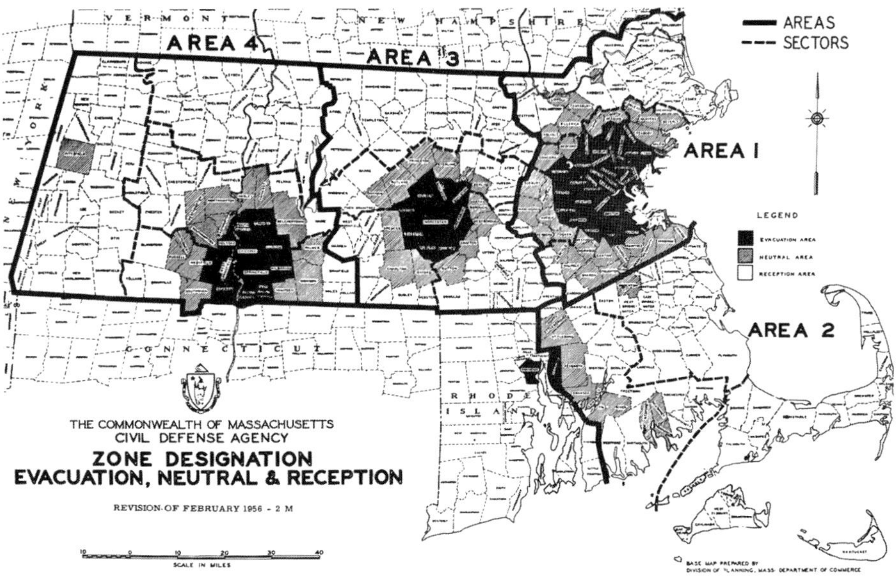

In 1956, the Massachusetts Civil Defense Agency distributed this map showing evacuation, neutral and reception zones, based on four civil defense regions, for public safety. *MEMA*.

shelters, which he referred to as a necessity, and advised heads of families to view these shelters as a form of insurance.

The first national fallout shelter survey began in early February 1962 in Boston and nearby communities. The aim was to identify public fallout shelters that could accommodate a minimum of fifty people and meet acceptable protection standards. This phase involved collecting information sources, determining peak population densities and selecting structures suitable for use as fallout shelters. Shelters were categorized as stocked, unstocked or makeshift refuge, meaning they did not meet the federal standard and should only be used as a last resort.

Governor Volpe initiated the second phase of the Home Fallout Protection Survey in 1968. This survey, conducted by the U.S. Bureau of the Census, focused on communities with populations of ten thousand or more. Its purpose was to identify the best possible shelter spaces in homes, using mailed questionnaires and personal visits by enumerators to collect detailed household information. This data was intended to assist in future planning and improve public safety measures and aimed to determine the feasibility and cost of enhancing the degree of protection, habitability and capacity of existing shelters.

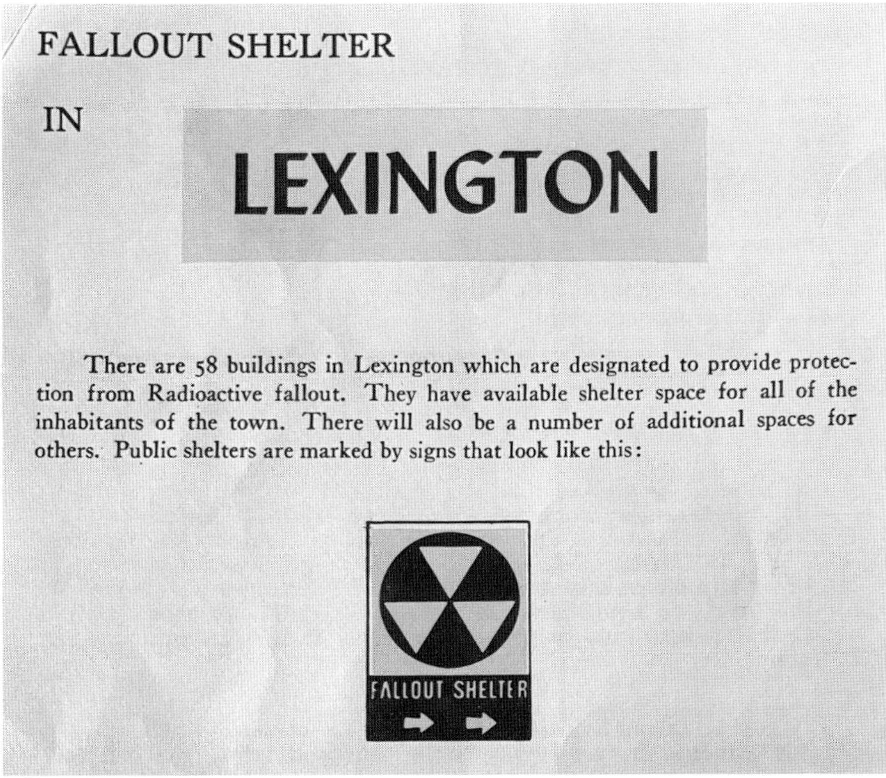
FALLOUT SHELTER

IN

LEXINGTON

There are 58 buildings in Lexington which are designated to provide protection from Radioactive fallout. They have available shelter space for all of the inhabitants of the town. There will also be a number of additional spaces for others. Public shelters are marked by signs that look like this:

In Lexington, fifty-eight buildings were designated fallout shelters, providing space for all residents. Shelters were marked by a distinctive yellow and black sign. *FalloutFiveZero.*

A 1999 article in the *Boston Globe* provided reflective insight into efforts to build fallout shelters across various Massachusetts communities following JFK's speech in October 1961. Each community in Massachusetts was taking on a community-wide effort at the municipal level. These individual and family shelters were in addition to that. The narrative revealed a mix of urgency, fear and practicality that drove many families and institutions to take extraordinary measures for protection against the perceived imminent threat of nuclear war.

In the summer of 1961, amid heightened Cold War tensions, President John F. Kennedy's call for Americans to build fallout shelters resonated deeply in Tewksbury. On Claire Street, seven families banded together, contributing $600 each to construct a cooperative fallout shelter. The ambitious project, costing $7,200 instead of the planned $4,200, resulted in a twenty-two-by-thirty-eight-foot underground shelter designed to accommodate fourteen adults and thirty-four children. However, what began as a symbol of community unity quickly disintegrated into disputes over provisions and plans for handling nonmembers in emergencies. By early December 1961, the shelter was complete, but the conflicts led some to question its viability.

Concord saw a different kind of response to the shelter-building frenzy. In 1961, local clergy voiced strong opposition to the construction of private fallout shelters. They argued that such shelters promoted a survivalist mentality, discriminated against the poor and distracted from the broader goal of preventing nuclear war. Their efforts highlighted the ethical and moral debates surrounding the fallout shelter movement during that period.

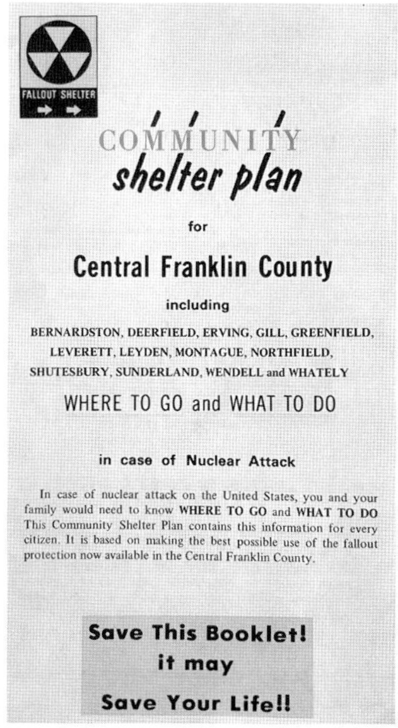

FALLOUT SHELTER

COMMUNITY
shelter plan
for
Central Franklin County
including
BERNARDSTON, DEERFIELD, ERVING, GILL, GREENFIELD, LEVERETT, LEYDEN, MONTAGUE, NORTHFIELD, SHUTESBURY, SUNDERLAND, WENDELL and WHATELY

WHERE TO GO and WHAT TO DO

in case of Nuclear Attack

In case of nuclear attack on the United States, you and your family would need to know WHERE TO GO and WHAT TO DO This Community Shelter Plan contains this information for every citizen. It is based on making the best possible use of the fallout protection now available in the Central Franklin County.

Save This Booklet!
it may
Save Your Life!!

Franklin County, Massachusetts, issued this booklet detailing shelter plans and safety measures for residents in the event of a nuclear attack, circa 1970. *FalloutFiveZero.*

Bedford's Russet Road was home to two underground shelters built in the early 1960s. These shelters were later integrated into house structures, serving as family rooms or garages. One homeowner noted persistent leaks, questioning the effectiveness of the shelters. Despite these issues, the shelters remain as concrete reminders of a time when nuclear fears dominated the public consciousness.

In Worcester, a family built a shelter beneath their home in 1961. A member of the family recalled the pervasive fear of the era. This sense of urgency and the looming threat of nuclear war drove many families to take drastic measures, even if such efforts seemed inadequate in hindsight.

In Cohasset, a resident built a secret fallout shelter in his basement in the early 1960s. He kept the shelter's existence a secret to avoid conflicts with neighbors in the event of a crisis. He later recalled the psychological toll and sense of urgency that prompted the shelter's creation, underscoring the intense fears that gripped many during that era.

Despite these efforts, public interest in building fallout shelters varied. A Smith College study in 1968 revealed that only one resident in

Northampton had constructed a shelter. Many respondents cited financial constraints or were undecided about the necessity of such shelters. Factors influencing public opinion included education level, religious beliefs and political affiliations.

Both sheltering and evacuation had their advantages and drawbacks. Sheltering offered immediate protection against fallout and was more feasible in urban areas. Evacuation was logistically complex and increasingly impractical with more powerful nuclear weapons. Civil defense efforts during the early Cold War reflected a balance between these approaches, influenced by technological advancements, political debates and public sentiment.

Military Bases and Hospitals: Supporting the Cold War Efforts

Hanscom

Hanscom Air Force Base, located in Bedford, Massachusetts, has been a crucial part of the United States' defense efforts, particularly during the Cold War era. Its history is closely connected to the development of advanced radar and communication systems, which have significantly influenced both military and civilian technology, highlighting Massachusetts's contributions.

Hanscom Field was initially established as the Boston Auxiliary Airport in 1941. This facility became essential to the U.S. military during World War II. However, its role in defense research and development began during the Cold War, a period marked by heightened geopolitical tensions and technological competition with the Soviet Union. The Soviet Union's nuclear weapons and long-range bombers capable of reaching the United States posed a significant threat, prompting the U.S. Air Force to develop the Semi-Automatic Ground Environment (SAGE) system. This comprehensive network was designed to detect and intercept Soviet bombers and represented a monumental leap in air defense technology, integrating radar detection with real-time data processing capabilities.

The SAGE system's development was closely linked with MIT's Lincoln Laboratory, established to address air defense challenges. The laboratory's origins trace back to concerns raised by George Valley, an MIT professor, about the inadequacies of U.S. air defenses against nuclear attacks. His

Three noncommissioned officers at the USAF Electronic Systems Division test communications equipment of the Hanscom Field Fallout Shelter Command Post. *MCDA*.

efforts, along with those of other scientists, led to the formation of the Air Defense Systems Engineering Committee (ADSEC), which played a crucial role in conceptualizing the SAGE system.

Radar was the backbone of SAGE. Hundreds of radar stations across the United States, including many in Massachusetts, formed a network that continuously scanned the skies for incoming threats. Data from these radars was transmitted to SAGE direction centers, where it was processed by AN/FSQ-7 computers. These computers, among the most advanced of their time, managed vast amounts of data and provided real-time responses to potential threats.

Hanscom Field's proximity to MIT and Lincoln Laboratory made it a key site for testing and demonstrating the SAGE system's capabilities. In September 1950, an experimental radar system at Hanscom successfully transmitted data to the Whirlwind computer at MIT, proving the feasibility of real-time radar data processing. This demonstration was a critical milestone in the development of SAGE and highlighted Hanscom's essential role in advancing air defense technology.

Throughout the 1960s and into the 1970s, Hanscom Air Force Base continued to lead radar and communication research. The base's Air Force Cambridge Research Laboratories (AFCRL) conducted significant research in meteorology, atmospheric physics and solar physics. However, the primary focus remained on radar and communication systems critical for national defense.

In 1967, AFCRL's research included the development of advanced radar calibration techniques and reentry communication studies. Notably, the Trailblazer II rocket experiment investigated the effects of high-temperature, shock-ionized flow fields on microwave transmissions. These studies were essential for improving the resilience of communication systems during reentry conditions, a critical aspect of missile and space vehicle operations.

Hanscom's contributions were not limited to radar technology. The base also played a significant role in developing communication systems that could withstand the harsh conditions of space and atmospheric reentry. For instance, the development of digital radar relays capable of transmitting data over telephone lines was a crucial advancement that enabled the real-time processing capabilities of the SAGE system.

Hanscom Air Force Base's innovations had far-reaching impacts beyond the immediate region. The advancements in radar and communication technologies developed at Hanscom contributed to national defense and had significant civilian applications. The modular computer architecture developed during the SAGE program, for instance, laid the groundwork for modern computing and was a precursor to technologies used in various industries today.

The establishment of Hanscom Field and its subsequent development into a premier research facility also spurred economic growth in the surrounding areas. The influx of scientists, engineers and military personnel led to the growth of local communities and contributed to the development of the Route 128 technology corridor, which became a hub for electronics and computer industries. This growth positioned Massachusetts as a leader in technology and innovation.

Hanscom Air Force Base's legacy is evident in its continued contributions to defense and technology. The base remains a critical site for research and development, supporting various programs that enhance national security. Its history reflects a broader narrative of technological advancement driven by the needs of national defense, illustrating how local efforts in Massachusetts have had profound national and global impacts.

Fourth Cliff

Fourth Cliff, located in Scituate, Massachusetts, has played a varied and evolving role in U.S. military history, particularly reflecting changes in military technology and strategy from World War II through the Cold War. Initially, during World War II, Fourth Cliff was utilized as a radio direction finding station. This installation was crucial for intercepting and analyzing enemy communications, which helped in gathering intelligence and improving the effectiveness of U.S. military operations. The strategic location of Fourth Cliff allowed it to monitor Atlantic communications and contribute significantly to naval and air defense efforts during the war.

As the Cold War escalated, the technological demands of national defense led to significant advancements in military capabilities at Fourth Cliff. Transitioning from its original role, Fourth Cliff was equipped with more advanced radar systems. These were not just for detection but also for the integration into a larger network of air defense systems. The installation became a part of the SAGE system, a cutting-edge network that linked radar

Fourth Cliff in Scituate was a World War II Radio Direction Finder Station, later hosting 1950s radio towers and becoming part of the SAGE network for air defense. *Digital Commonwealth.*

stations across North America to provide real-time data on airborne threats. This system used computers to process incoming radar data and facilitate a rapid response, such as scrambling fighter jets or launching missiles to intercept potential Soviet attacks. Fourth Cliff's radar capabilities were thus integrated into a continental network that aimed to provide a comprehensive shield against the threat of long-range bombers and other aerial threats during the Cold War.

With the dissolution of the Soviet Union and the diminishing threat of large-scale air attacks, the strategic importance of coastal radar stations like Fourth Cliff decreased. The site was eventually decommissioned as a military radar station. Today, Fourth Cliff is utilized as a military recreation facility, providing a retreat for military personnel and their families, showcasing its transition from a critical defensive outpost to a site of rest and recuperation. Throughout its operational history, Fourth Cliff has reflected the broader narrative of technological and strategic evolution in U.S. military history, adapting to the needs of the time from intense global conflict to periods of peace and restructuring.

Fort Devens

During the Cold War era, Fort Devens in Massachusetts emerged as a pivotal site for U.S. Army intelligence training and operations. Established in April 1951 as the U.S. Army Security Agency (ASA) school, Fort Devens provided comprehensive training in various intelligence disciplines. These included communications analysis, communications security, electronic intelligence, electronic warfare, Morse and non-Morse intercept and crypto-equipment maintenance. This specialization allowed Fort Devens to play a crucial role in Cold War military strategy, focusing on electronic intelligence and communications-related electronic warfare operations.

In 1955, the ASA's mission was redefined to include electronic intelligence and electronic warfare, responsibilities previously managed by the U.S. Army Signal Corps. This strategic realignment underscored the significance of electronic intelligence within the broader field of signals intelligence. As a result, Fort Devens became a central hub for developing and managing these critical intelligence functions, ensuring that ASA operatives were well trained in the latest techniques essential for Cold War espionage and surveillance.

Soldiers operate a mobile short-wave radio teletypewriter station during Operation Alert at Fort Devens, June 1954. It enabled communications between the army and FCDA office. *Digital Commonwealth.*

Fort Devens's role further expanded in 1967 when the Military Intelligence Branch was established, transforming from combat service support to combat support. This evolution highlighted the increasing importance of specialized, professional intelligence officers. Fort Devens significantly contributed to this shift by providing advanced training in electronic intelligence and electronic warfare, equipping personnel with the skills needed to navigate the complexities of Cold War espionage and surveillance.

The importance of Fort Devens continued to grow through the late 1970s and 1980s. On October 1, 1976, the U.S. Army Security Agency Training Center and School (ASATC&S) was redesignated as the U.S. Army Intelligence School Devens (USAISD), marking its transformation into a distinct institution. The curriculum was updated to emphasize tactical training and self-paced, performance-oriented learning. New training methodologies, such as simulators, extension courses, Skill Qualification Tests, Individual Training Plans, Soldiers Manuals and the Army Training

Evaluation Program, were introduced. These changes ensured that Fort Devens continued to produce highly skilled intelligence personnel capable of meeting the evolving demands of military operations.

On October 1, 1990, as part of the BRAC initiative, the U.S. Army Intelligence School Devens was closed, and training for these programs moved to Arizona. The final class graduated from USAISD on September 9, 1994.

Westover

Westover Air Force Base in Chicopee, Massachusetts, played a significant role in several key events and operations. Established in 1940, the base initially served as a training ground for bomber crews, conducted anti-submarine patrols and housed prisoners of war during World War II. However, its importance grew substantially in the postwar period, particularly during the Berlin Airlift in 1948, when it became a major support base.

The Berlin Airlift was a critical operation during the early Cold War, initiated in response to the Soviet blockade of West Berlin. The blockade cut off all ground access to the city, leaving its 2.5 million residents without essential supplies. Westover Air Force Base played a crucial role in this effort, with its C-47 and C-54 transport planes flying numerous missions to deliver food, fuel and other necessities. This operation, which lasted for 327 days, involved over 276,926 flights to Berlin. The local community supported the effort, most notably through Operation Little Vittles, where candy and small supplies were parachuted to Berlin's children.

General Curtis LeMay was a significant figure in American military history and had strong connections to Westover. He was the architect of the Berlin Airlift and later became known as the father of the Strategic Air Command (SAC). LeMay was stationed at Westover in the early 1940s and played a pivotal role in developing the strategies that defined America's Cold War military stance. He spearheaded the doctrine of massive retaliation, which aimed to deter Soviet aggression by threatening overwhelming nuclear response.

The Cuban Missile Crisis was a critical moment in the Cold War, bringing the world to the brink of nuclear war. Westover Air Force Base was integral to the U.S. response. It was at Westover that photographs taken by U-2 spy planes, which revealed Soviet nuclear missiles in Cuba, were developed in the highly secure Building P-1900. During the crisis, Westover's B-52 bomber crews were on high alert, ready to launch a nuclear response if

From 1948 to 1949, Chicopee's Westover Air Force Base served as a key support hub for the Berlin Airlift, known as Operation Little Vittles. *Chicopee Historical Society.*

necessary. This period underscored the base's strategic importance and its role in national security.

"The Notch," part of the SAC Post-Attack Command Control System (PACCS), was a top-secret bunker located in the Mount Holyoke Range, north of Westover. This subterranean facility, buried under two hundred feet of rock, was designed to survive a nuclear attack and ensure continuity of command. It served as a command center where the Eighth Air Force could direct its nuclear bombers in the event of an attack until it was relocated from Westover to Indiana. The existence of the Notch was a closely guarded secret throughout the Cold War, reflecting its strategic importance.

In 1956, Westover became a base for the Strategic Air Command, a key component of the United States' nuclear deterrence strategy. SAC's mission was to maintain a state of readiness, with bomber crews prepared to launch nuclear-armed B-52s at a moment's notice. Westover's selection as a SAC base underscored its critical role in America's defense strategy. The base

The Notch in Amherst, built in 1958, was a forty-thousand-square-foot bunker designed as the alternate command post for Westover Air Force Base. *Mark Foster.*

housed B-52 bombers and aerial refueling tankers, essential for maintaining long-range bombing capabilities.

The "Mole Hole" was a structure at Westover built to house crews of B-52 bombers on continuous alert. This facility, constructed in 1959, was part of SAC's strategy of massive retaliation. Bomber crews lived in the Mole Hole on twenty-four-hour alert, ready to launch at any time. The nearby runway, known as the "Christmas Tree," was where these bombers were positioned for rapid deployment. This setup was designed to ensure that the United States could respond quickly and effectively to any nuclear threat.

Stony Brook

Directly contiguous to but separate from Westover, Stony Brook Air Force Station, operational from 1954 to 1962, was a top-secret facility tasked with storing, maintaining and readying nuclear weapons for the Strategic Air Command. Established around 1953–54 and initially operating under the Air Materiel Command, the station's control shifted to SAC under Westover Air Force Base (WAFB) in July 1962.

Operating under a strict veil of secrecy, Stony Brook used code names such as "Site Item" and euphemisms like "Special Reporting Squadron" to describe its work. This intense secrecy was crucial for national security but also created an atmosphere of paranoia and fear. Personnel adhered to rigorous protocols, and one airman recounted being held at gunpoint for forgetting the daily password to enter a weapons storage facility.

One of thirty-two bunkers at Stony Brook AFS stored nuclear arsenals for B-52 Stratofortresses from Westover AFB. These grass-covered vaults ensured high security and concealment. *Photo by the author.*

Stony Brook AFS operated from 1954 to 1972, storing atomic weapon components. These bunkers are now horse stables for the Hampden County Sheriff's Office. *Photo by author.*

The base handled a variety of nuclear weapons, including the massive MK-17 thermonuclear bomb, the MK-6 similar to the "Fat Man" bomb dropped on Nagasaki and smaller tactical devices like the W-31 for the army's Nike Hercules surface-to-air missile. Maintenance involved meticulous inspection, testing and modification processes. Airmen became intimately familiar with these weapons, developing a sobering expertise. The constant threat of sabotage led to the "Two-Man Rule," requiring two qualified personnel to be present at all times when handling nuclear material.

Personnel received specialized training at Sandia Base, New Mexico, and later at Lowry AFB, gaining a comprehensive understanding of nuclear weapon systems. Stony Brook's physical layout featured two primary "Plants" (A and B) for weapons maintenance, numerous storage igloos, administrative buildings, barracks, a mess hall and a motor pool. Weapons were transported to WAFB via heavily guarded convoys using specialized vehicles like straddle carriers and NI/MF-1 trailers. A joint agreement outlined responsibilities between SBAFS and WAFB for weapons handling, security, transportation and communication.

Life at Stony Brook, despite the dangers and secrecy, had lighter moments. Airmen formed close bonds, organizing softball games and fishing trips and even building a makeshift NCO club in a barracks basement. However, the base's remoteness and demanding work schedule took their toll. The constant roar of B-52s taking off from nearby Westover AFB disrupted sleep and served as a stark reminder of the high stakes involved.

Security at Stony Brook was extraordinarily tight, involving multiple layers of clearance, daily passwords and armed guards. Despite these measures, breaches occurred, such as an incident where an individual attempted to gain access using a fake ID card. Safety was paramount, evidenced by stringent protocols, radiation monitoring and training programs emphasizing the destructive power of the weapons. One notable incident involved a runaway crane that damaged a training weapon, highlighting the potential for catastrophic accidents with live devices.

Cohasset Naval Magazine and Hingham Naval Ammo Depot

The Cohasset Annex is one of strategic importance, evolving from its critical role during World War II to a focal point of Cold War defense. Initially functioning as a navy ammunition depot from 1941 to 1962, the Annex

From 1956 to 1961, Nike-Ajax site BO-38 operated on the former Hingham-Cohasset Naval Ammunition Depot Annex, which contained three magazines for missile storage. *The Military Standard.*

played a crucial role in supplying ordnance to the Atlantic fleet. This effort was vital in the Battle of the Atlantic, aiding in the victory over Europe. At its peak in June 1945, the depot supported a workforce of 2,091 civilians, 721 naval officers and sailors and 375 Marine guards.

Among the 108 concrete bunkers in the Cohasset Annex, Bunker N9 stands out as the most significant element of Cold War history. In the 1950s, it became notable for housing the U.S. Navy's first nuclear depth charge. This transition marked Bunker N9's importance in the evolving landscape of military technology and defense strategies. These missiles, designed to counter the threat of enemy submarines, were compact and fit inside a box launcher commonly found on cruisers and destroyers. Each missile was approximately fifteen feet long and thirteen inches in diameter and weighed around a ton.

These weapons were transported to the Annex from the Quonset Point Navy base in Rhode Island in a six-vehicle convoy, guarded by U.S. Marines. From the Annex, the missiles were moved to the Hingham Naval

Ammunition Depot (now Bare Cove Park) and then shipped by barge to warships waiting in Boston Harbor.

By 2000, the original rockets were replaced by newer models. Additionally, the Annex contributed to producing the navy's first surface-to-air and air-to-surface missiles. The Cold War era saw Bunker N9 at the forefront of military preparedness, producing ordnance for conflicts like the Korean War and the Vietnam War. The last military activity at the Annex occurred when the U.S. Army Reserve 187th Infantry Brigade was stationed there from 1971 to 1982.

Maynard Ammo Depot (1942–82)

The Maynard Ordnance Storage Depot, also known as the Maynard Ammo Dump, played a crucial role during World War II. Established in 1942, the depot was part of the United States' efforts to improve logistics and supply chain efficiency, reflecting lessons learned from World War I. During that war, the U.S. military significantly improved its command-and-control structures, transport and distribution processes, enabling efficient mobilization and supply of troops and equipment across the globe. The depot at Maynard was integral to this system, serving as a key storage and distribution point for munitions destined for the European theater of war.

The initial phase of the depot, known as the Maynard Phase, began in the early 1940s when the U.S. government acquired the site and established it as the Maynard Ordnance Depot. Covering about 2,750 acres and including portions of Maynard, Hudson, Stow and Sudbury, the depot rapidly transformed from farmland to a critical military installation. During World War II, the depot constructed fifty earth-covered concrete igloos for ammunition storage. These igloos were designed to store large quantities of munitions safely, using reinforced concrete and earthen coverings to protect against fire, bomb impacts and aerial detection. The design included safety measures such as the capacity to direct internal blasts upward to minimize damage to neighboring structures.

After the war, the facility was renamed the Maynard Ordnance Test Station, focusing on ammunition storage, testing, disposal and related support activities. The depot's infrastructure supported these functions, ensuring that surplus munitions were managed safely and efficiently. In 1958, control of the annex was transferred to the U.S. Army Natick Research and Development Command (NARADCOM), marking the beginning of the

One of the fifty ammunition storage bunkers at Maynard Ammunition Backup Storage Point, which served as a military research test station. *Photo by author.*

Natick Phase. During this period, the facility was used by various agencies and operators for a wide range of purposes, including testing, training and waste disposal. This phase saw a diversification of activities at the depot, reflecting broader military and civilian needs during the Cold War era. Natick Labs conducted explosive and rocket tests in designated test and demolition areas, potentially leaving behind explosive residues, chemicals and unexploded ordnance (UXO).

The site housed several key installations, including an air force radar installation, which was crucial for national defense during the Cold War. Additionally, the Federal Emergency Management Agency (FEMA) established a Regional Operations Center at the depot, enhancing its role in national emergency preparedness and response. From 1958 to 1982, the Massachusetts Air National Guard and the 3245th Civil Engineers constructed an obstacle training course. The Natick Labs continued to use the site for field testing and storage activities, focusing on chemical substances until 1991.

In 1983, Fort Devens acquired custody of the entire annex, initiating the Devens Phase. This period saw the facility being used extensively for training by various state and federal agencies. The Massachusetts Fire Fighting Academy, Massachusetts State Police and Massachusetts Army and Air Guard reserve and active-duty units utilized the site for training exercises. The academy conducted flammable liquid training and car fire training, using two bermed fire pits filled with water and fuel oil for training purposes.

The Massachusetts State Police and NARADCOM also used the facility's bunkers for storage, leveraging the existing infrastructure to support their operations. The depot's strategic location and robust infrastructure made it an ideal site for these activities, ensuring that it remained a valuable asset for both military and civilian purposes. Transportation and logistics were critical components of the depot's operations. The Maynard depot was connected to the Central Massachusetts Railroad, operated by the Boston and Maine Company. This connection facilitated the efficient movement of large volumes of ammunition and other supplies, reducing the reliance on trucks, which were less efficient and posed greater safety risks.

The Central Massachusetts Railroad, established in the late nineteenth century, provided a vital link from the depot to broader national and international supply routes. This strategic rail connection ensured that the depot could effectively serve as a hub for the distribution of munitions, supporting the Boston Port of Embarkation. The Boston Port of Embarkation was a key port designated for the shipment of troops and supplies to various theaters of war, and the Maynard depot played a supporting role by ensuring that these supplies were ready and available for shipment.

In 1991, an assessment by the CDC found various contaminants at the Sudbury Training Annex, including explosive residues, chemical wastes, petroleum, oil, lubricants, pesticides, herbicides, PCBs and mustard agent. The site was subsequently remediated and is now the Assabet River National Wildlife Refuge, preserving its historical significance while repurposing the land for conservation.

South Weymouth Naval Air Station

Naval Air Station South Weymouth was established in 1942 during World War II. This period saw a significant increase in military infrastructure to support the war effort, and NAS South Weymouth was among seventeen blimp bases created to defend the U.S. coastline from German U-boats. Blimps, or lighter-than-air (LTA) craft, were particularly effective in this role because they could fly lower and slower than airplanes, allowing

This blimp collapsed at South Weymouth NAS on April 11, 1958, due to a heavy snow load. The base operated navy blimps from 1942 to the early 1960s. *Digital Commonwealth.*

for better monitoring of the coast. The station's two large LTA hangars, initially made of wood, were upgraded to steel and eventually to concrete over the years.

In the early 1950s, the base began transitioning from its original blimp operations to supporting jet fighters. Despite this shift, from 1954 to 1961, NAS South Weymouth housed the Naval Air Development Unit (NADU). NADU played a crucial role in testing classified electronic equipment for MIT Lincoln Laboratory and Raytheon. This unit was essential to the development of the SAGE air defense system, utilizing radar-equipped blimps for early warning radar (AEW) to detect potential air attacks.

Although blimps could remain airborne for long periods and move at slower speeds, which enhanced their ability to detect enemy aircraft from a distance, they ultimately proved inadequate as AEW-radar platforms due to their limitations in low-altitude flights. NAS South Weymouth was among the final U.S. locations where the navy operated blimps, including the N-class blimps built by Goodyear, which were the largest airships to fly.

After NADU was demobilized in 1961, NAS South Weymouth continued as a training facility. The base eventually closed in 1996, and the navy fully withdrew from the site in 1997.

North Truro AFS

North Truro Air Force Station (AFS) was established in December 1951 on a high coastal bluff with a strategic view of the Atlantic Ocean. This location, near the tip of Cape Cod, Massachusetts, was crucial for national defense. From its inception until 1985, the station was operated by the 762nd Radar Squadron. The site had initially served military purposes during World War II, housing U.S. Army Coast Artillery antiaircraft gun emplacements and several buildings.

The air force took over the site in 1948 and began constructing the radar station in early 1949. By November 1950, the 762nd Aircraft Control and Warning Squadron had been activated to manage the facility, which became operational in 1951. Initially equipped with a long-range search radar, the station faced limitations in tracking low-flying aircraft. Over time, newer radar technologies were introduced, improving capabilities to determine range, direction, altitude, speed and identification of aircraft.

In 1958, North Truro AFS became part of the SAGE system, which enhanced its ability to process and relay radar data crucial for air defense. The station also supported the "Texas Towers," offshore radar platforms that provided early warning information from 1955 to 1963. North Truro served as a staging area for supplies, spare parts and replacement crews, which were transported to the towers by helicopter. To support these operations, additional infrastructure, including a helicopter pad and supply buildings, was built. During this period, the station's staff, both military and civilian, increased to over five hundred people.

The station played a significant role in integrating radar data from various sources. It transmitted tracking information to the Ground Control Intercept (GCI) at Otis AFB, which combined this data with inputs from other radar stations, navy ships and the Ground Observer Corps. The information was manually copied onto plotting boards, which ground controllers used to direct defensive fighters to their targets, a process that was both slow and labor-intensive.

By the mid-1950s, the base had expanded to cover 125 acres, including operational buildings and a family housing area. It was largely self-sufficient, generating its own power, sourcing water from wells and operating its own sewage treatment plant. Despite its remote location, the station offered various recreational facilities such as a theater, bowling alley and sports fields.

The station was deactivated on June 14, 1985, although its height-finder radar continued operating until 1987. The Federal Aviation

Administration (FAA) then assumed control of the radar operations for tracking international flights. Portions of the station were transferred to the National Park Service and became part of the Cape Cod National Seashore. Today, the FAA still uses the site for air traffic control, continuing the station's legacy in national defense.

Antiaircraft Artillery Sites

The Massachusetts Army National Guard (MAARNG) played a pivotal role in the United States' air defense efforts during the mid-twentieth century. Their formal integration into the On-Site Air Defense Program on February 1, 1955, marked a significant transition from their traditional responsibilities as Coast Artillery units stationed primarily on the islands of Boston Harbor. These artillery units, which included the 9th, 211th and 241st Coast Artillery, were initially established and federally recognized in 1948. This integration represented a shift in focus from coastal defense to comprehensive air defense, responding to the evolving threats of the Cold War era.

The 704th AAA Battalion (90mm) trained at Camp Wellfleet, on Cape Cod, an adjunct of Camp Edwards. Built in 1942, it was used until 1961. *MAARNG.*

In the early 1950s, the U.S. Army recognized the increasing threat of aerial attacks, prompting the establishment of antiaircraft artillery units across the country, including Massachusetts. The MAARNG initially contributed units from the 704th AAA Battalion (90mm gun) and later the 772nd AAA Battalion (90mm gun). These units were crucial in operating sites armed with 90mm and 120mm guns designed to protect the Boston Air Defense Sector from potential enemy aircraft.

Training was a critical component of this transition. Members of the MAARNG underwent extensive training at the Antiaircraft and Guided Missile School at Fort Bliss in El Paso, Texas. This training included the use of M33 Radar Systems, 90mm guns and other related equipment. Camp Edwards in Massachusetts also served as a training ground, specifically for the 102nd AAA Brigade, ensuring that the National Guard units were well prepared for their new responsibilities.

The landscape of air defense began to shift dramatically in 1950 with the onset of the Korean War, which led to the establishment of the U.S. Army Antiaircraft Command (ARAACOM). Before this period, the United States had minimal antiaircraft artillery units actively engaged in air defense duties within its borders. The creation of ARAACOM signaled a heightened focus on domestic air defense, and the MAARNG's integration into the On-Site Air Defense Program was a direct response to this increased need for vigilance and preparedness.

Initially, the MAARNG used 90mm guns for air defense, a role they maintained until 1958. During this period, they served as an augmentation force supporting the active army's air defense efforts. The 90mm guns, positioned strategically around the Boston Air Defense Sector, formed a critical component of the region's protection against potential enemy aircraft. The presence of these guns not only provided a physical deterrent but also demonstrated a tangible commitment to the defense of the United States' Eastern Seaboard.

A significant turning point for the MAARNG's air defense capabilities occurred in 1958. The active army transitioned from the traditional antiaircraft artillery to the more advanced Nike missile systems. This transition allowed the MAARNG to take on new roles and responsibilities, operating missile sites that marked a new era in air defense technology.

The evolution of the MAARNG's air defense role from 1950 to 1958 highlights the dynamic nature of military strategy and technology during this period. The transition from traditional AAA gun sites to missile sites was driven by the need for more effective and sophisticated defense mechanisms.

The Belmont site in 1956, part of the army's Antiaircraft Artillery Gun Site Program, featured four 90mm AA guns. This program was the predecessor to Nike. *Digital Commonwealth.*

This evolution was not only a response to technological advancements but also a reflection of the changing nature of threats and the increasing importance of air defense in national security.

In 1957, the reclassification of AAA units to Air Defense Artillery marked another significant milestone. This change was part of a broader effort to streamline and modernize the army's artillery branches, ensuring that units were better equipped to handle the demands of modern warfare. The establishment of Air Defense Artillery as a distinct branch in 1968 further underscored the importance of this specialization within the army.

As the MAARNG transitioned to the operation of missile sites, their role in national defense continued to expand. The Nike systems, which would come to include the Nike-Ajax and later the Nike-Hercules, represented significant advancements in air defense technology. These systems allowed for greater range, higher altitude and faster response times, enhancing the overall effectiveness of the air defense network.

Nike Bases (Ajax and Hercules)

During World War II, the United States developed advanced military technologies and defense strategies that laid the groundwork for the Cold War era. Between 1955 and 1974, Massachusetts played a critical role in the United States' defense network through the deployment of Nike missile batteries, which were designed to intercept potential aerial threats.

Twelve Nike missile installations were established in the Boston Defense Area. Sites B-03 in Reading, B-15 in Beverly, B-17 in Nahant, B-55 in Blue Hills/Randolph and B-63 in Needham operated from the mid-1950s until March 1963. These installations each maintained one Nike Hercules missile battery, two Nike Hercules missiles, thirty Nike Ajax missiles and twelve launchers for the Nike Ajax missiles.

In Danvers, site B-05 had a longer service period, operating from November 1956 until April 1974. It hosted one Nike Hercules missile battery with two missiles, plus an additional eighteen in storage, thirty Nike Ajax missiles, twelve launchers for the Ajax missiles and seven launchers for the Hercules missiles. Hull's B-36 and Lincoln/Wayland's B-73 were also operational until 1974, each with two Nike Hercules missile batteries and twelve missiles. B-36 had twenty Nike Ajax missiles and eight launchers, while B-73 maintained the same number of Ajax missiles and launchers.

Weymouth's B-37 and Burlington's B-84 had two Nike Hercules missile batteries each. B-37, active from January 1956 until December 1961, contained twenty Nike Ajax missiles, whereas B-84, operational until August 1963, included eight launchers for the Ajax missiles.

Cohasset/Hingham's B-38 and Bedford's B-85, both functional from November 1956 until December 1961, each maintained one Nike Hercules missile battery, two Nike Hercules missiles, thirty Nike Ajax missiles and twelve launchers for the Ajax missiles.

A portion of the Providence Defense Area was situated in Massachusetts and included PR-19 in Rehoboth and PR-29 in Swansea. Both of these sites housed one Nike Hercules missile battery, two Nike Hercules missiles, thirty Nike Ajax missiles and twelve launchers for the Ajax missiles.

The Nike Ajax missile, which used highly corrosive liquid fuel, required special handling and closed-system draining before shipment to depots. While the Ajax missiles were cost-effective, they demanded more maintenance due to their fuel's corrosive nature.

The Nike Ajax missile's booster section, on display at the Massachusetts Army National Guard Museum, includes the booster rocket motor and large stabilizing fins used during the initial launch phase. *MAARNG Museum.*

Sergeant Frank R. Ferrara, firing panel operator at Battery D, enters the stairwell to the underground missile storage at the Reading Nike Launch Site. *MAARNG Museum.*

Nike Launch Site B-15 in Beverly, near the airport, operated from February 1957 to March 1963 with Ajax and Hercules launchers and thirty Ajax missiles. *Digital Commonwealth.*

These Cold War artifacts are staged in Beverly, outside the FEMA Massachusetts Task Force (MATF-01) headquarters, once the Nike Missile Launch Site (B-15). *Photo by author.*

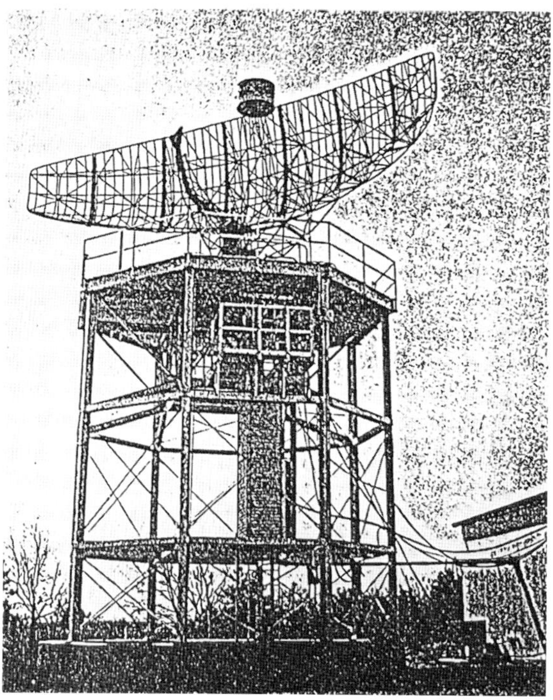

Above: An underground magazine room at Nike Launch Site B-15 was sixty by sixty feet, with a ten-foot ceiling supported by beams. A fifty-seven-foot-long missile elevator was centered in the room. *Photo by the author.*

Left: Alternate Battery Acquisition Radar (ABAR) antennas detected long-range targets, enhancing the Nike system's range. This unit was installed at the Lincoln Nike site. *MAARNG Museum.*

VIPs gathered for the unveiling of the Hercules Missile (*left*) at North Weymouth Missile Base on April 7, 1959, with a Nike Ajax in the background. *Digital Commonwealth.*

A soldier operates the control panel at Nike launch site B-85 in Bedford, active from November 1956 to December 1961. *Digital Commonwealth.*

Left: In 1956, soldiers load Nike Ajax missiles onto launchers at Bedford (B-85). The site is now owned by Harvard University. *Digital Commonwealth.*

Below: Soldiers in protective suits inspect a Nike antiaircraft missile at Bedford (B-85) launch site on November 21, 1956, ensuring readiness and safety protocols. *Digital Commonwealth.*

Two soldiers raise a Nike Ajax missile on the elevator from the underground magazine at Bedford launch site, November 21, 1956. *Digital Commonwealth.*

The Nike Hercules missile, which succeeded the Ajax, had a ninety-mile range and could reach speeds of Mach 3.6. It was capable of carrying a nuclear warhead, offering significantly increased capability and range. Both Ajax and Hercules missiles used the same launch facilities, though the Hercules was safer and easier to service. A monorail launcher, seven-ton steel structure with electrical and hydraulic components was utilized to launch the Nike Hercules missiles. Notably, Nike Ajax missiles could also be launched from this system.

Missiles were stored and transported in metal containers, fully assembled with boosters, fuel and warheads, and kept in underground magazines. No reserve missiles, boosters, fuel or warheads were stored on-site; replacements were brought in as needed. Launchers were oriented toward a designated Booster Disposal Area, calibrated to stop their tilt just short of vertical to ensure that the booster would land near the center of the disposal area under normal conditions.

Above: In 1959, Massachusetts Army National Guard's 241st Artillery took control of four Nike Ajax sites previously managed by the active army. *Photo by the author.*

Left: Soldiers inspect an Integrated Fire Control (IFC) area with surveillance radars for target identification, also known as acquisition radars. November 21, 1956. *Digital Commonwealth.*

The underground magazine room, used to store missiles, was a sixty-foot-by-sixty-foot space with a ten-foot-high ceiling supported by beams. A fifty-seven-foot-long missile elevator was positioned in the center, with its pit extending six and a half feet below the room's floor. Blast-resistant doors and a crew escape hatch provided additional security.

The U.S. Army Corps of Engineers New England Division, based in Waltham, managed the construction of these facilities. Some sites utilized existing Department of Defense property, such as World War II gun casements for missile control radars.

Initially, Regular Army troops manned Boston's Nike Batteries. In 1959, National Guard units took control of B-03, B-15, B-55 and B-63. By 1964, the army had transferred sites B-36 and B-73 to the Guard. After the Nike Ajax system was phased out, sites B-05, B-36 and B-73 continued to be supplied with Hercules missiles. Massachusetts Army National Guard units of the 1st and 2nd Missile Battalions, 241st Artillery, played a significant role in manning these sites.

Each Nike battery had its own acquisition and tracking radar facilities, allowing them to operate independently. However, they were typically coordinated through a fire direction system known as Missile Master, housed at Army Air-Defense Command Post (AADCP) B-21DC at Fort Heath, Massachusetts. This command-and-control center, operational from 1960, was integrated with the USAF Air Defense Command/NORAD SAGE air defense radar network and staffed by up to five hundred personnel, coordinating Nike batteries throughout the Northeast.

In 1962, the Boston Defense Area merged with the Hartford and Providence Defense Areas to form the New England Defense Area. Air force operations at Fort Heath ended in 1962, and Nike operations were inactivated in 1974.

These sites, with their advanced missile systems and strategic coordination with SAGE and AT&T Long Lines, helped protect key regions from potential aerial threats.

Otis Air Force Base and BOMARC (Otis, 1960)

Otis Air Force Base, located on Cape Cod, Massachusetts, played a significant role in the United States' military defense strategy during the Cold War. Established in the early twentieth century, Otis Air Force Base was initially used for training purposes and coastal defense. However, as geopolitical tensions escalated during the Cold War, its strategic importance grew. By the late 1950s, the base was selected as a primary site for the deployment of the BOMARC (Boeing and Michigan Aeronautical Research Center) missile system, a critical element in the nation's defense against aerial attacks.

The United States faced a constant threat of aerial attack from adversaries, prompting the U.S. Air Force to consider various defense mechanisms to protect national security. Among these was the BOMARC missile, a surface-to-air missile system seen as essential for national defense. The air force emphasized the necessity of deploying the BOMARC system as swiftly as possible, given the intense geopolitical climate of the time. In December 1957, the U.S. Air Force revealed plans to establish a BOMARC missile site at Otis Air Force Base, underscoring its strategic importance.

To meet this urgent demand, the New England Division of the U.S. Army Corps of Engineers was tasked with the rapid construction of BOMARC missile batteries. The urgency of the situation led to the selection of Otis Field as one of the primary sites for these installations. Construction at this site was expedited, and the batteries were completed and handed over to the air force between late 1959 and early 1960. This quick turnover underscores the pressure and importance placed on the BOMARC system by military strategists.

The initial deployment of the BOMARC missiles utilized liquid fuel propulsion, a technology that, while effective, posed several logistical and operational challenges. Liquid fuel is highly volatile and requires meticulous handling and storage procedures, making the missile system more complex to manage. Recognizing these issues, the air force decided to upgrade the BOMARC missiles at Otis Field to solid fuel propulsion shortly after their installation.

Solid fuel offered several advantages over liquid fuel, including greater stability, ease of storage and faster readiness. However, this upgrade necessitated significant modifications to the existing launcher facilities. The conversion process was undertaken with great urgency and was completed by February 1962. This modification period highlights the continual efforts to improve the missile system's reliability and effectiveness.

The construction of the BOMARC missile batteries was one of the most hastily executed projects of the Cold War, reflecting the perceived immediate threat and the corresponding need for rapid defense capabilities. Each missile site featured twenty-eight launcher shelters, meticulously designed and constructed from reinforced concrete. These

The BOMARC site at Otis was operational from 1959 until 1972. It was part of the Air Defense Command's strategy to use BOMARC missiles to intercept long-range Soviet bombers. *USAF.*

shelters measured approximately sixty feet in length, twenty-four feet in width and twelve feet in height, providing robust protection for the missiles housed within.

A key feature of these shelters was the large steel biparting doors installed on top. These doors, designed by Boeing, could be swiftly opened to raise a missile into its firing position in about ten seconds. This rapid deployment capability was crucial for maintaining a state of readiness and ensuring a prompt response to any aerial threats. The collaborative efforts between the army corps of engineers and Boeing were essential in ensuring the proper functioning of these doors, which included achieving weathertight seals to maintain a controlled climate within the shelters.

The BOMARC missile system was designed with formidable capabilities to defend against potential aerial attacks. The missiles were capable of carrying either nuclear or conventional warheads, providing flexibility depending on the nature of the threat. They were designed to strike targets up to four hundred miles offshore and at altitudes reaching seventy thousand feet, making them effective against a wide range of enemy aircraft.

One of the standout features of the BOMARC missiles was their rapid response time. The system was capable of launching a missile within thirty seconds of receiving an order, ensuring that enemy aircraft could be intercepted quickly. Additionally, the powerful explosives carried by the missiles did not require a direct hit to destroy enemy targets, further enhancing their effectiveness.

The public's reaction to the deployment of the BOMARC system, including its nuclear capabilities, was generally accepting. This acceptance was largely due to the prevailing trust in government decisions regarding national defense. Moreover, the potential for job creation associated with the BOMARC sites contributed to the public's positive reception. The deployment process, while complex, was managed efficiently to maintain public support and confidence.

Despite the advanced capabilities and strategic importance of the BOMARC missile system, it was quickly rendered obsolete by the rapid development of Intercontinental Ballistic Missiles (ICBMs). ICBMs offered greater range and destructive power, making them a more effective deterrent against potential threats. This swift obsolescence underscores the rapid pace of technological advancement during the Cold War and the continuous evolution of military strategies and capabilities.

The BOMARC sites, once seen as vital to national defense, were decommissioned in 1973. This marked the end of a brief but significant

Governor Herter narrowly escaped injury when a U.S. Air Force F-89 Scorpion crashed three hundred yards from his plane at Otis Air Force Base on July 2, 1956. *Digital Commonwealth.*

period in which the BOMARC missile system played a key role in the United States' aerial defense strategy. The decommissioning process involved dismantling the missile installations and repurposing the sites for other uses, reflecting the ever-changing landscape of military technology.

In the years following the decommissioning of the BOMARC sites, environmental concerns have arisen regarding the potential impacts of the missile system's operations. A 1998 test conducted at the former BOMARC site at Otis Air Force Base revealed no evidence of radioactive contamination. This finding provided some reassurance regarding the environmental safety of the site. However, this does not entirely eliminate the possibility of other environmental issues.

The operation and maintenance of the BOMARC missile system involved the use of various petroleum products and chemicals. These substances, if not properly managed, could pose environmental risks. Similar former military sites have faced significant challenges related to past waste disposal practices, highlighting the need for ongoing environmental monitoring and remediation efforts.

Otis Air Force Base was one of eight BOMARC sites in the country. These sites housed a total of 409 missiles. The locations of these sites, which were widely known and accepted by the public, also housed thousands of Genie, Falcon and Nike-Hercules missiles as part of the nation's defense strategy.

Woods Hole, Project Nobska and the Summer Study

In the summer of 1956, a significant gathering known as Project Nobska took place in Woods Hole, Massachusetts. This event brought together a diverse group of oceanographers, scientists, engineers and naval officers to address the pressing issue of the emerging threat posed by Soviet nuclear-powered submarines. Named after the Nobska Lighthouse at the entrance to the harbor at Woods Hole, the project included notable figures such as Nobel laureates, physicists and policy authors. Additionally, distinguished oceanographers from various prestigious institutions played pivotal roles in the discussions.

The objective of Project Nobska was to harness decades of advancements in ocean science to enhance the United States' anti-submarine warfare capabilities. The initiative focused on leveraging the latest technological and scientific discoveries to counter the Soviet submarine threat. Project Nobska's Summer Study was organized into subgroups, each addressing different aspects of undersea warfare and naval strategy. These subgroups examined various technical topics, including naval weaponry, submarine propulsion systems, navigation, communication and sonar technology. There was also an emphasis on improving offensive capabilities with advanced missile and torpedo technology. Additionally, the study explored strategic issues such as the protection of ships at sea, strategic use of the undersea environment, containment of submarines, defense of the continental United States and the implications of political trends on undersea warfare.

Over several weeks, the seventy-three participants engaged in numerous briefings and even experienced some time at sea aboard destroyers. By the end of the session, Project Nobska had produced a comprehensive two-volume report with fifty-one recommendations. These covered a wide range of areas, from the development of active and passive sonar to the future of anti-submarine warfare and the use of tactical nuclear weapons in naval engagements. Key recommendations included the continued development of both active and passive sonar technologies to enhance submarine detection and tracking capabilities; the exploration of smaller, more agile submarines equipped with advanced propulsion systems; consideration of the use of tactical nuclear weapons in naval warfare scenarios; and the strategic deployment of submarines for both defensive and offensive operations, including the potential for basing strategic weapons at sea.

One of the critical outcomes of Project Nobska was its impact on strategic decisions. Inspired by discussions about smaller-yield warheads, the navy decided to commit resources to the development of the Polaris missile. Furthermore, Nobska's recommendations on sonar technology influenced significant design changes in future U.S. submarines, leading to innovations such as placing sonars in the bow and relocating torpedo tubes amidships, which allowed for more powerful sonar systems. Despite some criticisms and perceived implementation challenges, Project Nobska established a legacy of close collaboration between oceanographers and the navy. It highlighted the essential role of scientific research in addressing national security challenges and set a precedent for future partnerships in oceanographic studies.

Throughout the Cold War, the partnership between WHOI and the U.S. Navy significantly advanced naval warfare and oceanographic research, shaping the future of undersea warfare. This collaboration also led to the development and operation of advanced research vessels, expanding scientists' abilities to explore and study the ocean. The enduring partnership between WHOI and the U.S. Navy was instrumental in advancing oceanographic science and ensuring national security through innovative research and technology development.

SHIFTING FOCUS

FROM BOMBS TO POWER PLANTS

Nuclear Threats: Radiation and Emergency Planning Zones

Atoms for Peace

President Eisenhower's December 8, 1953 "Atoms for Peace" speech to the United Nations came shortly after the Soviet Union detonated its first hydrogen bomb on August 12, 1953, emphasizing the need for the peaceful use of atomic energy in the wake of escalating nuclear arms developments. Eisenhower's initiative spurred research advancements in nuclear power and medicine, with Massachusetts playing a pivotal role through contributions from institutions such as Massachusetts General Hospital (MGH) and the Massachusetts Institute of Technology (MIT) fostering scientific progress and the peaceful application of atomic energy.

In 1958, MIT established a research reactor funded in part by the Atomic Energy Commission (AEC). This facility became a central hub for training and research in nuclear engineering, advancing civilian nuclear technology and educating future nuclear scientists and engineers. The MIT Research Reactor (MITR) was instrumental in materials testing, neutron activation analysis and medical isotope production. Additionally, MIT's Nuclear Engineering Department, also founded in 1958, became a leader in promoting the peaceful uses of nuclear energy through education and collaborative research projects with government and industry partners. These efforts ensured that advancements in nuclear technology were widely disseminated and applied, supporting the goals of the "Atoms for Peace" program. MITR is still in operation today. James R. Killian served as MIT president from 1948 until 1959 and was involved in several projects that supported both military and energy projects. He served as special assistant for science and technology to Presidents Eisenhower and Kennedy during pivotal moments in Cold War history. In that capacity, he is often credited with laying the groundwork for the creation of NASA.

Massachusetts General Hospital was another key player in this era, leveraging the "Atoms for Peace" initiative to advance medical research and treatment using nuclear technology. The hospital received radioisotopes from the AEC that were used to develop new diagnostic techniques and therapies, particularly for cancer. From 1955 to 1956, more than a dozen doctors, researchers, military officers and educators from Massachusetts participated in radioisotope techniques courses at the Oak Ridge Institute of Nuclear Studies (ORINS) in Tennessee, gaining intensive training in handling and applying radioisotopes for research. This training was part of a broader effort to promote the peaceful use of nuclear technology worldwide and facilitated significant advancements in nuclear medicine in Massachusetts but made impacts around the country.

The use of medical isotopes at MGH led to the development of modern diagnostic imaging techniques, such as PET scans, and targeted radiation therapies that were more effective and less invasive than previous methods. These innovations significantly improved the accuracy and effectiveness of cancer diagnostics and treatments, establishing nuclear medicine as a crucial tool in modern medical practice. MGH also hosted training programs to educate healthcare professionals on the safe and effective use of radioisotopes, contributing to the development of a skilled workforce capable of leveraging nuclear technology for medical benefits.

In addition to the contributions from MIT and MGH, the "Atoms for Peace" program led to various public education initiatives. One notable example was the exhibit at the Museum of Science in Boston in November 1956, which showcased the benefits of nuclear energy for civilian purposes. This exhibit included models of nuclear reactors; informational displays on the applications of nuclear energy in medicine, agriculture and industry; and interactive components to engage visitors. The exhibit aimed to demystify nuclear technology and make it more accessible to the general public, aligning with the goals of the "Atoms for Peace" program.

The exhibit toured throughout the late 1950s in a large walkthrough bus, providing insights into the mining, processing and production of uranium and the structure of the atom. It included explanations of energy release from atoms and a model of a nuclear power plant, such as the one powering the submarine *Nautilus*. Visitors could see actual samples of uranium ore and metal, reactor components, food preserved by radiation and working Geiger counters. A trained exhibit manager was available to answer questions, ensuring an informative experience for all attendees. The exhibit visited various locations, including Westfield in 1958 and Agawam in 1960, educating the public about the peaceful uses of nuclear technology.

Yankee Rowe (1956/1961–1992)

The Yankee Rowe nuclear power plant's development was rooted in the World War II era's scientific advancements and geopolitical dynamics. Post–World War II, the Cold War catalyzed technological progress, particularly in nuclear energy, amid global tensions. This historical backdrop set the stage for President Eisenhower's "Atoms for Peace" program, which aimed to promote peaceful nuclear technology.

In 1954, eleven New England electric utilities formed the Yankee Atomic Electric Company to build a prototype nuclear power plant under this program. The Yankee Rowe plant, situated in Rowe, Massachusetts, began construction in 1958 and was completed by 1960. Originally planned for a six-year operational lifespan, it began commercial operations in 1961 and exceeded expectations by operating for over three decades.

Yankee Rowe was the first nuclear power plant in New England, producing 185 megawatts of electricity and playing a crucial role in the region's energy infrastructure. Throughout its operational life, it generated 44 billion kilowatt-hours of electricity, earning a reputation for reliability and safety globally.

The plant was designed to enhance atomic energy advancements and boost Rowe's local economy. With a construction cost of $35 million, it was set to generate 135,000 kilowatts of electricity through a nuclear chain reaction in a shielded furnace, producing steam to power generators. The facility comprised three primary industrial buildings: the reactor, turbine units and auxiliary buildings, including a probable pumping station.

Located on the Deerfield River's east bank, the plant site was selected for its remoteness and accessibility to the New England power grid. The

Above: The Yankee Rowe Nuclear Power Station, announced in 1956 and opened in 1961, operated until 1991 in Rowe, Massachusetts, along the Deerfield River. *USDOE.*

Left: The Massachusetts Civil Defense Agency distributed this booklet in 1982 to address common questions about radiation and nuclear power plants. *UMass–Amherst Libraries.*

architect's design, approved by the Atomic Energy Commission, emphasized functionality and minimal visual intrusion, with three main buildings and a dome-shaped extension housing either the reactor or furnace. The AEC granted preliminary approval based on comprehensive safety and operational plans, including stringent radioactive material handling measures.

Yankee Rowe significantly impacted the local economy and community, creating jobs and fostering a strong bond between the plant and residents. Despite occasional protests from anti-nuclear activists, the overall sentiment in Rowe remained supportive. The U.S. Nuclear Regulatory Commission (NRC) closely monitored the plant's operations, ensuring adherence to safety standards, which became a source of community pride.

By 1991, surrounding communities, including Shelburne and Ashfield, sought inclusion in the official emergency planning zone, reflecting ongoing safety concerns. State and local officials, along with the Massachusetts Emergency Management Agency (MEMA), emphasized the adequacy of existing emergency plans while recognizing the need for continuous review.

In February 1992, Yankee Rowe was shut down due to economic viability issues, and the decommissioning process began, concluding in 2007. The NRC confirmed the site was fully decommissioned according to federal regulations, shifting focus to the safe storage of spent nuclear fuel on-site.

During decommissioning, the plant continued to contribute to the local economy through employment and economic activity related to site maintenance and spent fuel storage. This phase introduced new challenges, particularly in infrastructure maintenance and emergency preparedness.

A significant challenge arose in 2019 when Rowe officials sought funding to repair the deteriorating road leading to the former plant site. The road was crucial for emergency access and spent fuel transport, with repairs estimated at $800,000. This financial burden was challenging for Rowe, which was already managing other significant infrastructure projects.

Town officials appealed to state and federal lawmakers for support, stressing the critical need for road maintenance due to the presence of radioactive spent fuel. Maintaining the road was essential for safety and future contingencies, underscoring the plant's long-term impact on the community. The 2019 edition of the MEMA Radiological Emergency Response Plan has a few references to Yankee Rowe, noting only the Independent Spent Fuel Storage Installation there. There is no Export Processing Zone (EPZ) around the Yankee Rowe plant.

Andover

In December 1956, the Sylvania-Corning Nuclear Corporation announced plans to build a new atomic plant in West Andover. This venture aimed to construct a multimillion-dollar facility on a 150-acre site. The center was designed to feature five buildings in a campus-like layout, focusing on the development and production of nuclear fuel elements and components while also advancing atomic energy research.

The project, called the "Andover Approach," was expected to cost between $4 and $5 million initially, with the total investment projected to reach $20 million. Employment at the facility was anticipated to start with three hundred workers, expanding to between eight hundred and one thousand within five years. The plant was intended to be operational by late 1958, and it was seen as a significant step in establishing New England as a leader in atomic energy development.

However, despite the ambitious plans and initial optimism, the project faced significant economic challenges. Dr. Lee L. Davenport, president of Sylvania-Corning Nuclear Corporation, announced the decision to cancel the project. Economic conditions impacting the nuclear industry, such as reduced government projects, underdeveloped peacetime uses and a competitive overseas market with less stringent regulatory procedures, were cited as the primary reasons for the abandonment.

The cancellation marked a significant setback for the region, which had been poised to benefit from the employment opportunities and economic boost that the plant would have provided. The project, once envisioned as an outstanding facility of its kind globally, was no longer feasible under the prevailing economic conditions.

Massachusetts's Response to Nuclear Power

Montague (1973)

In the early 1970s, Massachusetts was actively expanding its nuclear energy infrastructure, reflecting the era's ambition for technological progress and energy self-sufficiency. The Yankee Rowe plant in Rowe, which began operations in 1960, was the oldest and smallest nuclear station in New England with a capacity of 175 megawatts electric (MWe). Another significant facility

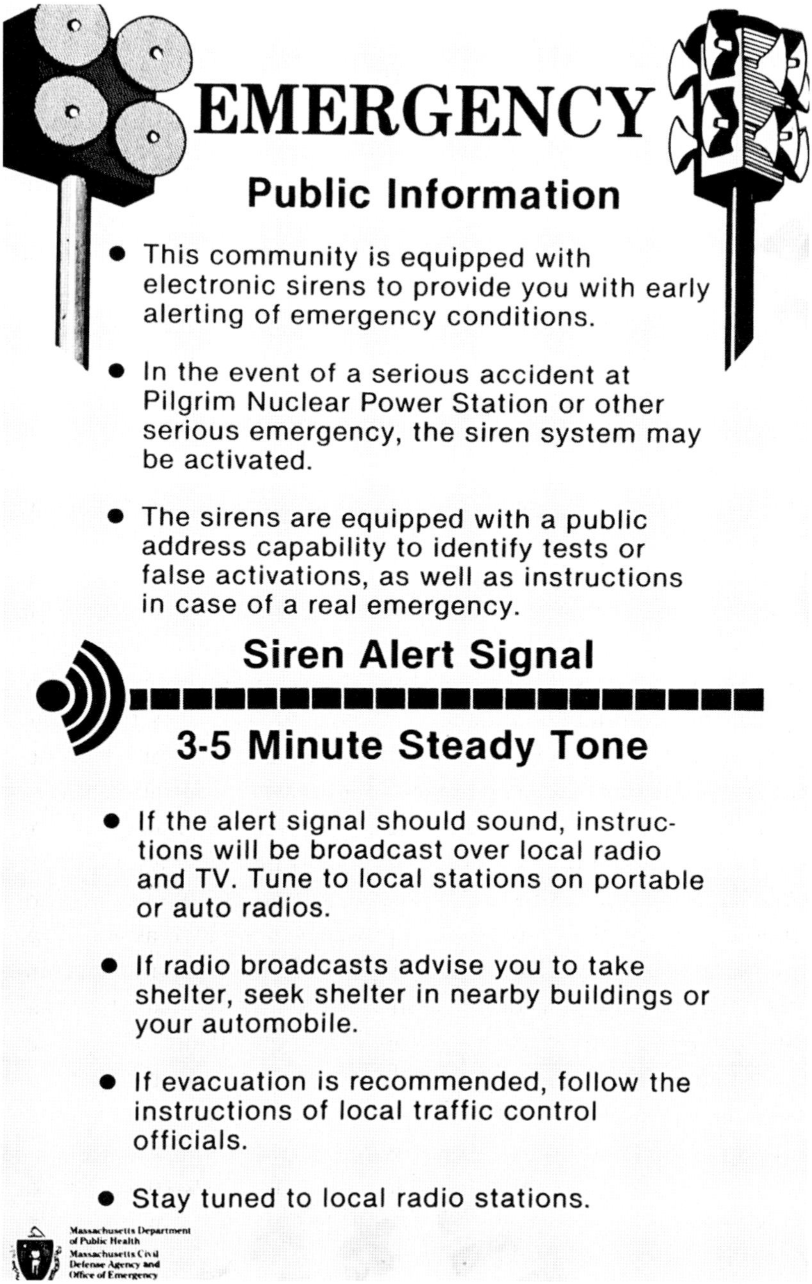

The Pilgrim Nuclear Power Plant, operational from 1972 to 2019, faced numerous issues. In 2010, it was rated the second most vulnerable in the United States. *MEMA*.

was the Pilgrim 1 plant in Plymouth, a 655-MWe unit that started operating in December 1972. Pilgrim 1 was part of a broader vision by Boston Edison Company to develop a three-unit complex, indicating a substantial commitment to nuclear energy.

Plans for further expansion were underway. Pilgrim 2 and Pilgrim 3 were projected to supply 1,180 and 1,150 megawatts, respectively, although Pilgrim 3 faced deferrals. In addition to these, Northeast Utilities intended to build two 1,150-MWe twin reactors in the rural town of Montague, located in western Massachusetts. These proposed Montague plants were expected to be a major economic boost, generating electricity for the region while providing jobs and potentially reducing local unemployment.

Despite the significant economic potential of these projects, they were met with considerable controversy and opposition. Proponents of nuclear power argued that such development was crucial for meeting the region's energy demands and ensuring economic growth and emphasized that nuclear power was a necessary and efficient solution to the rising energy needs of New England, offering a reliable source of electricity while promising economic benefits such as job creation and reduced unemployment.

However, opponents of nuclear power raised serious concerns about the safety and environmental impact of these plants. Critics highlighted the dangers of radiation, the potential for catastrophic accidents and the long-term consequences of nuclear waste. This growing opposition was part of a larger national discourse on the balance between technological progress, economic development and environmental protection. The complexities and challenges of addressing energy needs in a way that considered both the benefits and potential risks of nuclear power became increasingly apparent.

In February 1974, Samuel H. Lovejoy, a local farmer and environmental activist, dramatically opposed Northeast Utilities' plans by dismantling a five-hundred-foot weather tower on Montague Plain. This tower was crucial for gathering data needed for the nuclear project's approval. Lovejoy believed nuclear power posed severe environmental and safety risks, aiming to delay the project and raise public awareness. After dismantling the tower, he turned himself in, highlighting his commitment to civil disobedience. Lovejoy's protest became a symbol of the anti-nuclear movement, drawing national attention and sparking a highly publicized trial where he argued his actions were morally justified. Despite mixed public reactions and some labeling his actions as extreme, Lovejoy's protest underscored the broader opposition to nuclear power development in the community.

Ultimately, the plans for the nuclear power plant in Montague were abandoned in 1980. The project faced numerous delays and mounting opposition from local residents and environmental activists. The significant public resistance, combined with changing economic conditions and increased regulatory scrutiny following incidents such as the Three Mile Island accident in 1979, led to Northeast Utilities' decision to halt the project permanently. This decision marked a victory for the anti-nuclear movement and underscored the growing skepticism and caution surrounding nuclear energy development during that period.

PART II

★

MODERNIZATION AND CHALLENGES

THE MODERNIZATION OF CIVIL DEFENSE AND MILITARY ASSETS

Advancements in Warning and Communication Systems

Whirlwind

In the mid-twentieth century, technological advancements in computing began to revolutionize various fields. One of the most significant early developments in this domain was the Whirlwind project, initiated at the Servomechanisms Laboratory at the Massachusetts Institute of Technology. Commissioned by the Office of Naval Research, Whirlwind was initially conceived as a flight simulator that could accurately replicate the performance of all existing aircraft. This ambitious endeavor aimed to create a real-time digital computer, an unprecedented concept at the time.

Despite its promising beginnings, the flight simulator project faced numerous challenges, including budgetary constraints and technical difficulties. The situation took a decisive turn following the Soviet Union's successful test of an atomic bomb in 1949, which heightened the urgency for advanced air defense systems in the United States. George Valley, an associate professor in the MIT Physics Department, became deeply concerned about the effectiveness of U.S. air defenses in light of this new threat. His position on the U.S. Air Force Scientific Advisory Board (SAB) allowed him to assess radar stations firsthand. His observations, coupled with discussions with colleagues, underscored the nation's vulnerability to a nuclear attack. Recognizing the potential of Whirlwind's real-time computing capabilities, Valley took it upon himself to strengthen U.S. air defenses. The air force, through the Valley Committee, formally known as the Air Defense Systems Engineering Committee (ADSEC), integrated the project into their broader air defense strategy.

Initially, the Whirlwind project was driven by the navy's need for advanced flight simulation, providing early funding and the foundation for the project's development. However, the escalating Cold War tensions and the growing nuclear threat highlighted by the Soviet Union's atomic bomb test in 1949 led to a reassessment of U.S. air defense capabilities. This prompted the air force to seek technological solutions for a more robust air defense system. The convergence of these needs and Whirlwind's real-time computing capabilities, which were almost nonexistent in the batch processing world of the time, made the project an ideal candidate for integration into the air force's air defense strategy.

Whirlwind's technical advancements were groundbreaking. Initially, the computer had limited memory, with only five words of random access memory (RAM) and twenty-seven words of programmable read-only memory (ROM). Despite these constraints, its speed and 16-bit word length made it suitable for real-time data processing. By 1950, the Whirlwind team had successfully demonstrated the computer's ability to transmit radar data via telephone lines, allowing real-time analysis and direction of intercept missions. This was a pivotal moment, proving that real-time control was feasible and practical. One of the most significant contributions of the Whirlwind project was the development of magnetic-core memory. This technology, which vastly improved the reliability and speed of computers, became a cornerstone of future computing advancements. Magnetic-core memory was later adopted by IBM, and the IBM 704 mainframe computer, released in 1955, was the first nonmilitary system to utilize this innovation.

Whirlwind's success in real-time computing laid the foundation for the Semi-Automatic Ground Environment air defense system. SAGE was developed in response to the increasing threat posed by Soviet nuclear bombers. The Whirlwind computer served as an experimental test bed for this system, demonstrating the feasibility of real-time air defense control. By the spring of 1952, Whirlwind I had demonstrated sufficient functionality to be incorporated into the early stages of SAGE development. At that time, Whirlwind I resembled a "breadboard" more than a refined prototype for a fully operational air defense system. Consequently, the focus within the

Digital Computer Division shifted toward developing a production-ready computer, designated as Whirlwind II, later renamed AN/FSQ-7 using air force nomenclature. In April 1953, IBM was awarded the contract to design this new computer. The first prototype AN/FSQ-7, intended to replace Whirlwind I, was completed by January 1955.

The AN/FSQ-7, completed in January 1955, was a marvel of its time. Weighing 250 tons and requiring 49,000 vacuum tubes, it had a 3,000-kilowatt power supply. To ensure continuous operation, each system was duplexed, meaning it consisted of two interconnected machines. This massive computing power was essential for the real-time processing needs of the SAGE system, which coordinated air defense operations across North America.

MIT's involvement in the Whirlwind project extended beyond mere research and development. The institution's role evolved significantly with the establishment of Lincoln Laboratory in 1951. Although Lincoln Laboratory operated with a degree of autonomy, it remained closely tied to MIT, leveraging the university's research expertise to address national defense challenges. Lincoln Laboratory's Digital Computer Division, which absorbed the Whirlwind project, continued to operate in the Barta Building on Massachusetts Avenue and the Whittemore Building on Albany Street. This setup facilitated seamless collaboration between researchers and the ongoing development of advanced computing technologies.

The Whirlwind project was not just a technological milestone but also a strategic turning point in the history of computing and national defense. The initial impetus from the navy provided the foundation, while the air force's subsequent involvement steered the project toward addressing critical defense needs. MIT's pivotal role, particularly through the establishment of Lincoln Laboratory, ensured that the project had the necessary resources and expertise to succeed. Whirlwind's legacy is evident in its numerous technological contributions. The development of real-time computing, magnetic-core memory and the successful implementation of these technologies in the SAGE system had far-reaching implications. These advancements laid the groundwork for modern computing systems and demonstrated the potential of digital technology in complex, real-time applications.

The Whirlwind project stands as a testament to the power of collaboration between academic institutions, the military and private industry. It highlights how initial research efforts, driven by specific needs, can evolve to address broader and more urgent challenges. Through the combined efforts of MIT, the navy and the air force, Whirlwind not only achieved its original goals but also paved the way for future innovations in computing and defense technology.

SAGE

The SAGE air defense system was a monumental undertaking, surpassing even the scale of the Manhattan Project. It aimed to defend the United States against potential air attacks during the Cold War. The system relied on an extensive network of radars to detect enemy aircraft, transmit data to direction centers for analysis and coordinate interceptions by fighter jets or missiles. Massachusetts played a crucial role in its development and implementation, reflecting the state's contribution to broader national defense efforts.

The origins of the SAGE system can be traced back to the early 1950s. By 1952, experts were increasingly concerned about the vulnerability of North America's air defense, particularly the threat of Soviet bombers approaching undetected across the fifty-fifth parallel. This led to the concept of a radar network stretching from Alaska to Greenland, designed to provide comprehensive early warning and response capabilities.

In 1953, the Cape Cod System prototype was initiated in Massachusetts, covering a smaller radar network to test the feasibility of automated air defense. This prototype included long-range radars in South Truro, Massachusetts; Brunswick, Maine; and Montauk Point, New York, alongside gap-filler radars to ensure thorough coverage. By 1957, the Cape Cod System had successfully demonstrated detection and interception capabilities, marking a pivotal milestone in the SAGE project's development.

Building on this success, the Experimental SAGE Subsector (ESS) was developed, incorporating the AN/FSQ-7(XD-1) computer. This phase emulated a full-scale operational subsector, further proving the system's effectiveness. As a result, Lincoln Laboratory's focus shifted from research and development to operational testing and production.

The fully realized SAGE system comprised several key components. Hundreds of radars, including AN/FPS-3 long-range radars and smaller gap-filler radars, provided extensive coverage across the United States. Advanced radars like the AN/FPS-31, with a large 120-foot-wide antenna, offered improved performance by reducing clutter. The Texas Towers, radar installations on platforms in the Atlantic Ocean off the East Coast, extended coverage even farther. The Distant Early Warning (DEW) Line, a network of radar and communication installations across northern Canada, provided early warning of potential attacks from over the North Pole. Additionally, airborne early warning radar systems mounted on aircraft such as the Super Constellation enhanced detection capabilities beyond the reach of ground-based radars.

Twenty-four direction centers were equipped with AN/FSQ-7 computers, each capable of processing data from multiple radars and providing real-time guidance to interceptors. These centers featured over one hundred operator stations, each equipped with display consoles to monitor the air situation and control various system aspects. Three combat centers oversaw operations, allocating resources and coordinating responses across multiple direction centers.

The SAGE project spurred significant technological advancements, particularly in computing and software engineering. The AN/FSQ-7 computer, developed from MIT's Whirlwind computer, was a leap forward in real-time data processing. It utilized magnetic-core memory, an innovation by Jay Forrester, which significantly improved reliability and speed. This technology later became fundamental to the commercial computer industry. The system's software, with over 500,000 lines of code, pushed the boundaries of programming, leading to major advancements in software engineering. The development of interactive display consoles with light guns and keyboards for control was groundbreaking for its time and paved the way for modern human-computer interaction.

The development of the SAGE system was a collaborative effort involving multiple agencies and organizations. The United States Air Force played a central role in commissioning, funding and overseeing the SAGE project, with the Department of Defense tasking it with improving the nation's air defense in response to the Soviet nuclear threat. The air force sought the assistance of the Massachusetts Institute of Technology, leading to the formation of MIT Lincoln Laboratory, which became central to the SAGE project. Lincoln Laboratory designed the system architecture, prototyped key technologies, developed software and conducted field tests. The MIT Servomechanisms Laboratory, initially home to Project Whirlwind, provided the technological basis for SAGE's data processing capabilities. This lab later evolved into the MIT Digital Computer Laboratory and was eventually absorbed by Lincoln Laboratory.

International Business Machines (IBM) was selected as the primary contractor for building the AN/FSQ-7 computer, translating the experimental Whirlwind technology into a deployable system. The SAGE contract significantly contributed to IBM's growth as a major computer manufacturer. To manage the enormous software development demands, the air force contracted the Rand Corporation, leading to the formation of Rand's System Development Division, which later became the independent, nonprofit System Development Corporation. Western Electric was contracted to build and operate the DEW Line, extending SAGE's early warning capabilities. As the SAGE project transitioned from research and development to implementation, the MITRE Corporation was established in 1958 to take over the systems engineering responsibilities from Lincoln Laboratory.

By 1957, Lincoln Laboratory had largely completed its role in the SAGE project, transitioning the system to other organizations for implementation and operation. The legacy of SAGE extended beyond its immediate goal of air defense, leaving a lasting mark on the world of computing, software engineering and technological innovation. The SAGE program spurred the growth of the American computer and electronics industry, leading to the formation of companies like Digital Equipment Corporation (DEC). The software development challenges of SAGE led to breakthroughs in programming practices and the establishment of rigorous documentation procedures. The system also laid the groundwork for modern automated air defense systems, with many of its technologies evolving into systems used today.

The SAGE system's extensive network included numerous key locations. Twenty-four direction centers, each housing a dual AN/FSQ-7 computer system, were geographically dispersed across the United States. Hundreds of radar stations, including early warning and gap-filler radars, fed data into the direction centers. Three combat centers oversaw operations, coordinating responses across multiple direction centers. The direction centers were connected to hundreds of airfields and surface-to-air missile sites, enabling a layered defense strategy.

The Cape Cod System prototype included long-range radars in South Truro, Massachusetts; Brunswick, Maine; and Montauk Point, New York, along with gap-filler radars. Stretching across northern Canada from Alaska to Greenland, the DEW Line provided early warning of potential attacks from the north. Three radar platforms stationed in the Atlantic Ocean off the coasts of Cape Cod, Massachusetts, and Long Island, New York, extended the radar warning system farther out to sea. The SAGE system also utilized AEW aircraft equipped with UHF radar systems, including modified Super Constellations, to patrol coastal areas and enhance early detection capabilities.

The SAGE air defense system was a groundbreaking project that significantly advanced air defense capabilities during the Cold War. Massachusetts played a pivotal role in its development, contributing to broader national defense efforts and fostering technological innovations that had lasting impacts on computing, software engineering and air defense systems. The collaborative efforts of various agencies, academic institutions and private corporations were essential to the project's success, highlighting the interconnected nature of large-scale defense initiatives.

ESS in Massachusetts

Experimental SAGE Subsector in Massachusetts featured a network of critical radar sites operated by MIT Lincoln Labs, which significantly advanced radar technology and military defense capabilities.

One of these key sites was Pine Hill ESS (1952–60), located at the highest point on Cape Cod, 306 feet above mean sea level, on the west side of the Camp Edwards Military Reservation. This gap-filler radar location was essential for the ESS operations.

Similarly, Nantucket (1952) hosted a gap-filler radar and height-finding radar site, contributing to the experimental subsector's mission.

Otis Air Force Base (1960–72) served as Base No. 3 for the IM-99A BOMARC ground-air transmitter (GAT) and was notable for being the home base for the Texas Towers, part of an offshore radar defense network.

In Westborough (1957–62), a radar site atop Fay Mountain added to the network of ESS installations across Massachusetts.

The Scituate site (1952–60), located atop Coleman Hill, also functioned as a gap-filler radar location, enhancing radar coverage and defense strategy.

Chilmark (October 1952–58) on Martha's Vineyard further supported the ESS network, providing additional radar coverage in that region.

The Fall River ESS (1952) included a gated fire lane, playing a specific role in the subsector's operations.

The Sagamore Hill Solar Radio Observatory in Hamilton helped avert military escalation by identifying solar events that mimicked radar jamming, preventing false alarms of hostile actions. *Digital Commonwealth.*

At the MITRE Test Site on Boston Hill (1959), near North Andover, Massachusetts, a broadband radar was developed to test techniques against electronic jamming and passive countermeasures, pushing the boundaries of radar technology.

Another MITRE Test Site was located in South Truro (1955), continuing the trend of significant radar experimentation and development.

Halibut Point (1952–60), also known as Rockport, hosted a gap-filler radar and height-finding radar, mounted on an existing World War II coastal fire-control tower, blending old and new military technologies.

Additional sites within the Experimental SAGE Subsector included Chatham ESS (1952–60) and Clinton ESS (1952–64), each contributing to the broader radar defense efforts in Massachusetts during this period. These sites collectively enhanced the nation's radar coverage and defense capabilities, reflecting the significant advancements in technology and strategic military planning of the time.

Texas Towers and North Truro Station

As part of the ESS network, extending coverage further, the U.S. government embarked on an ambitious project: building a network of offshore radar stations in the Atlantic Ocean. These stations, known as the Texas Towers, represented a technological and engineering marvel, extending the nation's early warning capabilities hundreds of miles out to sea.

The Texas Towers were inspired by offshore oil-drilling platforms, characterized by their massive steel structures built to endure the North Atlantic's harsh conditions. Texas Tower 2, situated 110 miles east of Cape Cod, Massachusetts, was a pivotal component of this network. From May 1956 until January 1963, Texas Tower 2 operated with advanced AN/FPS-3 and AN/FPS-6 radar systems, designed to detect and track aircraft over long distances. The 762nd Aircraft Control and Warning Squadron, based at the North Truro Air Force Station in Truro, Massachusetts, manned the station, tasked with providing early warning of potential Soviet air attacks.

Life aboard Texas Tower 2 was grueling. The isolation and relentless Atlantic storms made conditions difficult for the men stationed there. A storm in November 1955 underscored the challenges and dangers of this mission. During this fierce storm, fifty-two personnel, including air force and navy members and civilian contractors, were trapped on the platform for days as hurricane-force winds and fifty-foot waves battered the structure.

Despite these treacherous conditions, the tower's robust construction ensured it withstood the storm.

This 1955 storm illustrated the Texas Towers' strategic importance and inherent vulnerability. Despite their critical role in national defense, the towers' exposure to severe weather made them precarious assignments. The severe Atlantic storm of January 1963, which led to the destruction of Texas Tower 2 and the loss of twenty-eight lives, highlighted these risks dramatically. This disaster prompted a thorough reassessment of the Texas Tower program, ultimately leading to its discontinuation.

Texas Tower 2 extended East Coast radar coverage, providing crucial additional time to react to potential threats. Its operations were supported by the North Truro Air Force Station, located on the Cape Cod National Seashore in Massachusetts. Established in 1951 by the U.S. Army Corps of Engineers, this station was initially part of the Air Defense Command (ADC) radar network, playing an essential role in monitoring and protecting U.S. eastern airspace.

PAVE PAWS (Otis, 1978)

By the 1960s, the Soviet Union had begun deploying submarine-launched ballistic missiles (SLBMs) from submarines patrolling the oceans, bypassing polar route defenses. The first Soviet SLBM was launched in 1955 from a diesel-powered submarine on the surface, but it had limited range. As the Soviet Union advanced technologically, it commissioned modern nuclear submarines capable of carrying SLBMs with greater range and reliability. By the late 1960s, these submarines presented a new threat that required the United States to rethink its defensive strategy.

The United States initially deployed a conventional radar detection system to address the SLBM threat. This system included seven radar sensors along the U.S. coasts, operational by 1971. These radars had limited range and capabilities, highlighting the need for a more advanced system. In response to the limitations of conventional radar systems, the United States began developing a new radar system in 1973. This new system utilized phased array radar technology, representing a significant advancement over mechanical radar systems. Phased array radars use a stationary array of antennas to electronically steer the radar beam, allowing for rapid detection and tracking of multiple objects with greater precision.

One of the first two sites for this new radar system was constructed at Otis Air Force Base in Massachusetts (later renamed Cape Cod Air Station). Construction was completed by 1978, and the site became operational in 1979. Cape Cod Air Station was strategically significant as the first U.S. site designed to detect SLBMs. The facility included a radar system housed in the Technical Facility/Scanner Building. This radar provided coverage for a three-thousand-mile area, including the Atlantic, Caribbean and northwest Arctic Ocean regions, and could detect objects as small as ten square meters and track components as small as one square meter.

Phased array radar technology allowed for significant improvements in missile detection and tracking capabilities. Unlike earlier radars, which had limited range and could track only single objects, the phased array system could simultaneously detect and track multiple targets with high precision. The radar faces, measuring approximately one hundred feet by one hundred feet, were highly sensitive and could adjust their focus nearly instantaneously. Cape Cod Air Station was heavily secured, with a perimeter fence monitored by armed security personnel, cameras and motion detectors. Security forces were on duty 24/7, constituting about 25 percent of the station's personnel. All buildings within the restricted area were constructed on an elevated concrete pad and clad with light beige metal paneling for durability and camouflage.

Cape Cod Air Station's radar system was crucial to U.S. missile defense during the Cold War. As the first U.S. SLBM early warning radar, it was designed to provide early detection and tracking of ballistic missiles aimed at North America. Its strategic location and advanced technology made it a key component of the nation's defense infrastructure. The phased array radar technology used at Cape Cod was a significant engineering achievement, allowing for electronic steering of the radar beam and tracking of multiple targets simultaneously. This advancement enhanced missile detection capabilities and contributed to strategic stability during the Cold War.

After the Cold War, the operations of these radar sites changed significantly. Some sites, such as those in Texas and Georgia, were partially dismantled as the threat landscape evolved. However, the Cape Cod Air Station's radar system remained operational, continuing to provide critical early warning and tracking capabilities. The facility's historical and engineering significance was recognized with its inclusion in the National Register of Historic Places, highlighting its importance in the Cold War and its contributions to national defense.

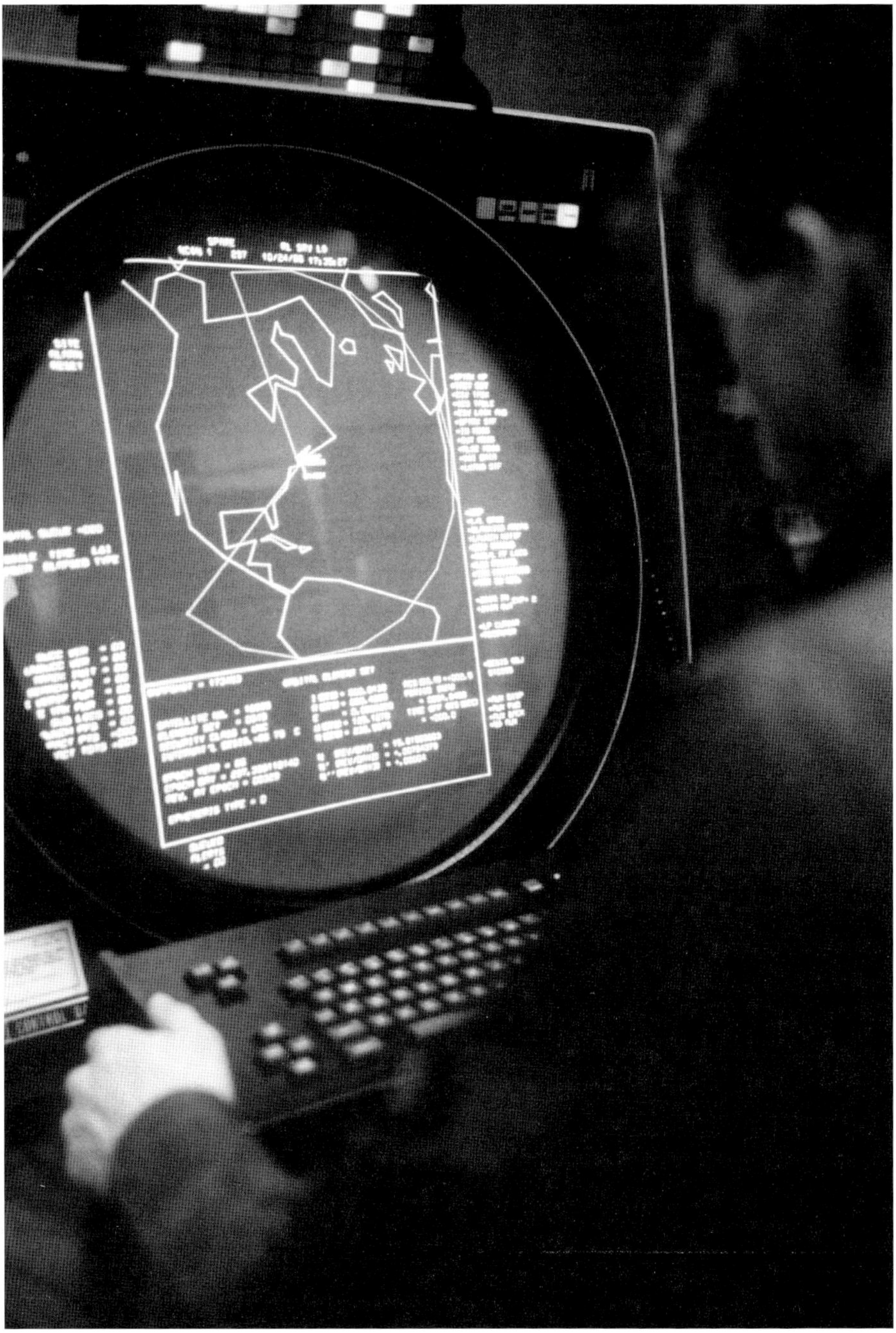

The PAVE PAWS radar screen at Cape Cod Air Force Station, October 1986. This system detected missile launches from submarines in the Atlantic Ocean. *U.S. Air Force.*

The development and deployment of this radar system were part of a larger U.S. effort to enhance missile defense capabilities. This system was connected to other radar and early warning projects, such as the Ballistic Missile Early Warning System (BMEWS). BMEWS, operational since the late 1950s, was the first ballistic missile detection and tracking system deployed by the United States. However, it relied on mechanical radar technology and had limited capabilities compared to phased array systems. In the late 1980s, two of the three BMEWS sites were upgraded to phased array using the new radar design, enhancing their capabilities.

The construction of the Cape Cod radar facility was led by an engineering team that included Raytheon. The facility's design incorporated several common characteristics of phased array radar structures, including size, geometric shape, construction materials and array placement. Phased array radar systems require immense electrical power and have maximum ranges of 2,400 to 3,600 miles, compared to typical long-range aircraft detection systems with ranges of around 240 miles. The antennas for missile detection are much larger, some measuring up to one hundred meters wide. The radars at Cape Cod were designed with future upgrades in mind. The array pattern of the radar face was circular, with densely packed antenna elements at the center and less dense elements toward the edges. Not all antenna elements were initially active, but they could be connected to wave tubes or power as needed, allowing for increased capabilities over time.

The radar system at Cape Cod Air Station is a critical component of the United States' missile defense strategy, developed in response to the evolving threats of the Cold War. Its advanced phased array radar technology, strategic location and robust security measures made it a vital asset for early warning and missile tracking. Throughout its history, the Cape Cod radar facility has played a significant role in maintaining strategic stability and enhancing the nation's defense capabilities. Its continued operation and recognition as a historically significant site underscore its enduring importance in U.S. military history and technological innovation. As of 2021, the site serves as the Cape Cod Space Force Station, continuing its legacy in national defense and space surveillance.

Communications

In 1947, AT&T introduced a pioneering microwave radio relay system connecting New York City and Boston. This technological leap enabled the transmission of large volumes of information, including multiple simultaneous conversations, over long distances using microwave technology. The system was essential to the Bell Telephone System's network, facilitating long-distance telephony and television transmission.

The terminal points were located at AT&T's headquarters in New York City and the New England Telephone and Telegraph Company's building in Boston. The microwave signal traveled in eight segments between these terminals, utilizing seven intermediate relay stations positioned approximately thirty miles apart on hilltops to ensure an unobstructed line-of-sight path necessary for microwave transmission. Each relay station was equipped with directional microwave antennas to transmit and receive the microwave beam, ensuring strong signal transmission across the distances involved. These stations were outfitted with emergency power supplies and other essential equipment to maintain uninterrupted service.

Planning and survey work for the project began in December 1943, requiring extensive fieldwork to identify suitable hilltops for the relay stations. The final route followed a zigzag pattern to minimize interference between adjacent relay stations, with construction involving over thirteen thousand feet of new roads and upgrading existing ones to ensure year-round access for maintenance and repairs. The system became operational in sections, culminating in the complete system opening to the public on November 13, 1947.

Asnebumskit Hill in Paxton, Massachusetts, was significant for facilitating network television broadcasts and long-distance calls. Waltham also played a crucial role as part of the initial 1947 microwave network, serving as an integral link in the broader AT&T Long Lines network.

In 1951, AT&T established the Long Lines network, a vital component of the United States' telecommunications infrastructure, supporting civilian and military communications. Initially relying on coaxial cable systems, the network transitioned to microwave relay towers to address the vulnerabilities and high maintenance costs of the former. The first coast-to-coast automated telephone call using the microwave system was made on August 17, 1951, marking a significant milestone in telecommunications.

During the Cold War, the Long Lines network's importance grew due to its strategic military applications. Relay towers equipped with line-of-sight horn antennas transmitted signals over long distances, connecting military installations and supporting national defense operations. Many relay stations were constructed underground in fortified locations to withstand nuclear attacks, equipped with shielded rooms to protect against electromagnetic pulses and survival kits to ensure continuous operation during emergencies.

Western Electric, a subsidiary of AT&T, manufactured the equipment for the Long Lines network, ensuring high quality and integration with military systems like the Semi-Automatic Ground Environment system used for air defense. The network's robustness made it ideal for transmitting military communications and data, with IBM utilizing the system for confidential purposes, highlighting its reliability.

In addition to military uses, the Long Lines network played a significant role in civil defense. Its ability to transmit television signals proved crucial for disseminating information quickly during crises, with television networks like NBC and CBS using the system for emergency broadcasts.

Technological advancements in the 1970s, particularly fiber optics and satellite communications, eventually rendered the Long Lines system obsolete. By the early 1990s, AT&T had decommissioned the network, with some towers being abandoned or repurposed.

Massachusetts played a crucial role in the nationwide microwave relay system, serving as a hub for nearly fifty AT&T sites. These sites, constructed in the late 1940s and early 1950s, ranged from simple antenna bases to hardened underground bunkers designed to withstand nuclear attacks.

In 1963, key Automatic Voice Network (AUTOVON) hubs were established in Massachusetts, including Blackstone, Chesterfield, Littleton and Peru. These hubs connected military installations across the state, enabling rapid communication during crises.

Constructed in 1966, Blackstone was an underground facility housing an AUTOVON switch, linking other sites and Westover Air Force Base. It played a significant role in carrying general toll circuits and crucial military communication circuits, extending its reach to transatlantic cables landing in Green Hill, Rhode Island. This two-story underground hardened building was manned twenty-four hours a day, serving as a metropolitan junction station and power center for the Boston–Miami route.

A hardened below-grade facility, Chesterfield provided AUTOVON services to military users such as Westover AFB, Barnes ARB and the Post Attack Command and Control System (PACCS) Facility in Hadley. This site terminated four separate communication routes and was equipped with three diesel generators to ensure reliable power. Chesterfield was designated as the secure relocation site for Julie Nixon, President Nixon's daughter, during her time at Smith College. The site, originally designed to withstand catastrophic events, has since been converted to industrial use.

In 1995, the Chesterfield bunker was purchased. The west concrete wall was exposed by excavation, and windows, doors and a loading dock were added. *Photo by author.*

Built in 1964, this subterranean Chesterfield facility supported circuits linking military bases and civilian traffic. The reinforced concrete structure covered about forty thousand square feet. *Photo by the author.*

Built in 1964, Littleton initially served as the AUTOVON provider for the New England region. It acted as a vital link between Blackstone and Boston and the Federal Regional Operations Center in Maynard. The site originally housed a switch that was later updated in 1988. Although the system was turned off in 1993 and replaced by fiber optics, the facility remains a critical node with a tall tower supporting a radio link to Sanford, Maine, and three gas turbines for emergency power.

Constructed around 1956 and upgraded in 1963, Peru featured an underground area with specialized equipment to offer protection against nuclear incidents, along with emergency power and protection against nuclear, biological and chemical threats. As a Ground Entry Point (GEP) site, Peru was a key relay point in the microwave path up the East Coast, connected to the Notch via a microwave link through Chesterfield.

Foxborough's High Rock AT&T site was another semi-hardened facility crucial to AT&T's operations in the region. It served as a central point for major microwave routes leading into Boston, including a single cable connection from Blackstone.

Located on Military Road in Amherst, the PACCS Facility the Notch provided the air force's Strategic Air Command (SAC) commanders with a shelter to conduct operations before and after an attack. PACCS operations on the ground were paralleled with an airborne command post aircraft based at Westover AFB, five miles south of this facility. In 1970, PACCS was relocated from Westover AFB to Grissom AFB, Indiana. Communications were provided by private cable and microwave to Chesterfield and Springfield. A two-hundred-foot tower sat on top of the bunker and supported a microwave link to the Chesterfield Communications site. A fifty-foot microwave tower on top of the mountain still exists, used to relay television conference calls between the base commander at Westover and the battle staff at the Notch.

The PACCS system was established by the Kennedy administration to better control the nation's nuclear firepower. The PACCS system consisted of aircraft equipped with command and control facilities that could serve as a command post if ground-based facilities were destroyed.

The Notch had four redundant communications paths (two microwave and two buried cable). One microwave path was from the top of the mountain to Westover AFB to the south, and the second microwave path was to the northwest to Chesterfield and Peru. Two buried cable routes also existed. The southern route went underground to Westover AFB and then to the Springfield central office. The northern buried cable route went to Amherst, where it entered a cable vault and then connected to the AUTOVON switch at Chesterfield.

The Automatic Voice Network was conceived in the early 1960s to enhance military communication capabilities. The system was designed to provide a high-capacity, secure telephone network that could function effectively during national emergencies and routine operations. The introduction of AUTOVON marked a significant advancement in military communications, allowing for the rapid and efficient transmission of information.

AUTOVON's capabilities extended beyond basic communication. The system featured touchtone phones with additional buttons for different priority levels, allowing high-priority calls to preempt lower-priority ones. This prioritization was crucial during emergencies, ensuring that critical communications could take place without delay. One of AUTOVON's notable achievements was its survivability, engineered to withstand enemy attacks and natural disasters. The system incorporated alternate routing facilities and predetermined restoration plans, ensuring communication could be maintained even in adverse conditions.

Hanscom Air Force Base in Bedford, Massachusetts, became a central hub for AUTOVON's development and implementation. The Electronic Systems Division (ESD) was established at Hanscom in 1961, marking the beginning of the base's pivotal role in the project. The ESD oversaw the design, construction and maintenance of the AUTOVON infrastructure, working closely with other military and civilian agencies to ensure the system's success.

Logan Airport in Boston was scheduled to be connected to the AUTOVON system, further enhancing the network's reach within the state.

Westover Air Force Base in Chicopee, an important Strategic Air Command base, was another key site in the AUTOVON network. In the early 1960s, Westover began leasing AUTOVON lines from commercial telephone companies exclusively for military use.

Barnes Airport, home to the 104th Tactical Fighter Group, was slated to be connected to the AUTOVON network in the mid-1960s. This connection aimed to integrate Barnes Airport with other military installations on the AUTOVON circuit, enhancing military readiness and coordination.

The history of the AT&T and AUTOVON networks in Massachusetts reflects a broader narrative of technological innovation and strategic importance. From the pioneering microwave radio relay system connecting New York City and Boston to the establishment of the Long Lines network and the strategic AUTOVON hubs, these networks played critical roles in advancing both civilian and military communication capabilities. Massachusetts's involvement in these networks underscores its pivotal role in the evolution of telecommunications infrastructure in the United States.

Civilian Defense

Federal Civil Defense Agency at Maynard

The Federal Emergency Operating Center was intended to be a civil defense initiative during the height of the Cold War. Construction commenced in October 1966 and concluded in March 1968. Situated in Maynard, Massachusetts, the structure was strategically embedded into a hillside, entailing the creation of a two-story reinforced concrete building covered afterward with earth to bolster its defensive properties. The construction was completed at a cost of $1.3 million and aimed to create a fortified environment capable of withstanding potential nuclear threats. The project was managed by the U.S. Army Corps of Engineers, ensuring rigorous standards in both construction and operational capabilities.

The design of the facility was the work of Praeger, Kavanagh, and Waterbury of New York, while Metcalf and Eddy of Boston served as engineers and architects. The general contractor for the project was the Edward R. Marden Corporation of Allston.

The bunker spans approximately thirty thousand square feet, designed to offer comprehensive protection from radioactive fallout and equipped with air filtration systems, medical facilities and a sophisticated communications network. This network included advanced telecommunications systems supported by multiple backup units, essential for maintaining operation during isolated conditions. The facility was equipped to accommodate and support operations for up to three hundred personnel, complete with its own power and water supplies, dormitories and a fully equipped kitchen.

The Region 1 Office of Civil Defense (OCD) and Office of Emergency Planning (OEP) headquarters moved to the bunker from Harvard, Massachusetts, on April 15, 1968, marking the start of its operational phase. The bunker also housed other critical federal agencies such as the Federal Communications Commission (FCC), the U.S. Army Corps of Engineers (USACE) and the American Red Cross (ARC), thereby

Above: The Emergency Operating Center in Maynard, Massachusetts, was built underground between 1966 and 1968 to serve as the Federal Civil Defense center for New England. *USACE.*

Left: The Region I headquarters of the Federal Civil Defense Administration in Harvard, Massachusetts, served as the New England nerve center from 1956 to 1968. *Digital Commonwealth.*

centralizing emergency response and civil defense operations within a single, fortified location.

Operational by April 1968, the bunker was designed to safeguard and manage the safety of thirty-six million people within its jurisdiction, which included multiple states and territories. The facility's robust construction and comprehensive facilities made it a pivotal component of the national defense infrastructure, capable of enduring severe conditions brought on by nuclear fallout and other emergencies.

Today, the facility continues to function under the auspices of FEMA, retaining its critical role in national defense and emergency operations. Its ongoing operational status underscores its effectiveness and enduring importance in fulfilling national security functions.

Massachusetts Civil Defense Agency State Emergency Operations Center (1963)

The Massachusetts Civil Defense Agency State Emergency Operations Center (SEOC), today known as the Massachusetts Emergency Management Agency bunker, was developed during the early 1960s. This initiative was part of President John F. Kennedy's vision to ensure the continuity of state government operations in the event of a nuclear war or other major disasters. The facility in Framingham, Massachusetts, was the first of its kind under this initiative and was completed and dedicated in November 1963, just days before Kennedy's assassination.

Constructed with reinforced concrete, the Bunker was designed to withstand the pressures of a twenty-megaton nuclear explosion occurring three miles away. The facility's walls and roof were covered by compacted earth and a parking area. This engineering allowed the structure to move with the blast force and return to its original position. The entrance ramps were built in a *Z* shape with ninety-degree turns to prevent radiation from entering, ensuring that radiation, which travels in straight lines, would be absorbed or stopped by the thick concrete walls. Additionally, mushroom-shaped air intake tunnels were installed to protect the ventilation system from radioactive fallout.

The SEOC was built to be entirely self-sufficient, capable of operating independently for up to thirty days. It could support a staff of three hundred people with its own heating, ventilation, lighting, water supply, food storage, cafeteria and sleeping facilities. It featured comprehensive communication systems linking it with local, state and federal agencies, as well as media outlets, ensuring efficient coordination during emergencies. The facility included advanced monitoring capabilities with direct communication to nuclear power plants and other critical infrastructure.

During emergencies, the SEOC served as the nerve center for disaster response, housing various state agencies, utility companies and public affairs groups. It coordinated the efforts of all relevant entities to ensure resources were directed where needed to manage crises effectively. The SEOC was not

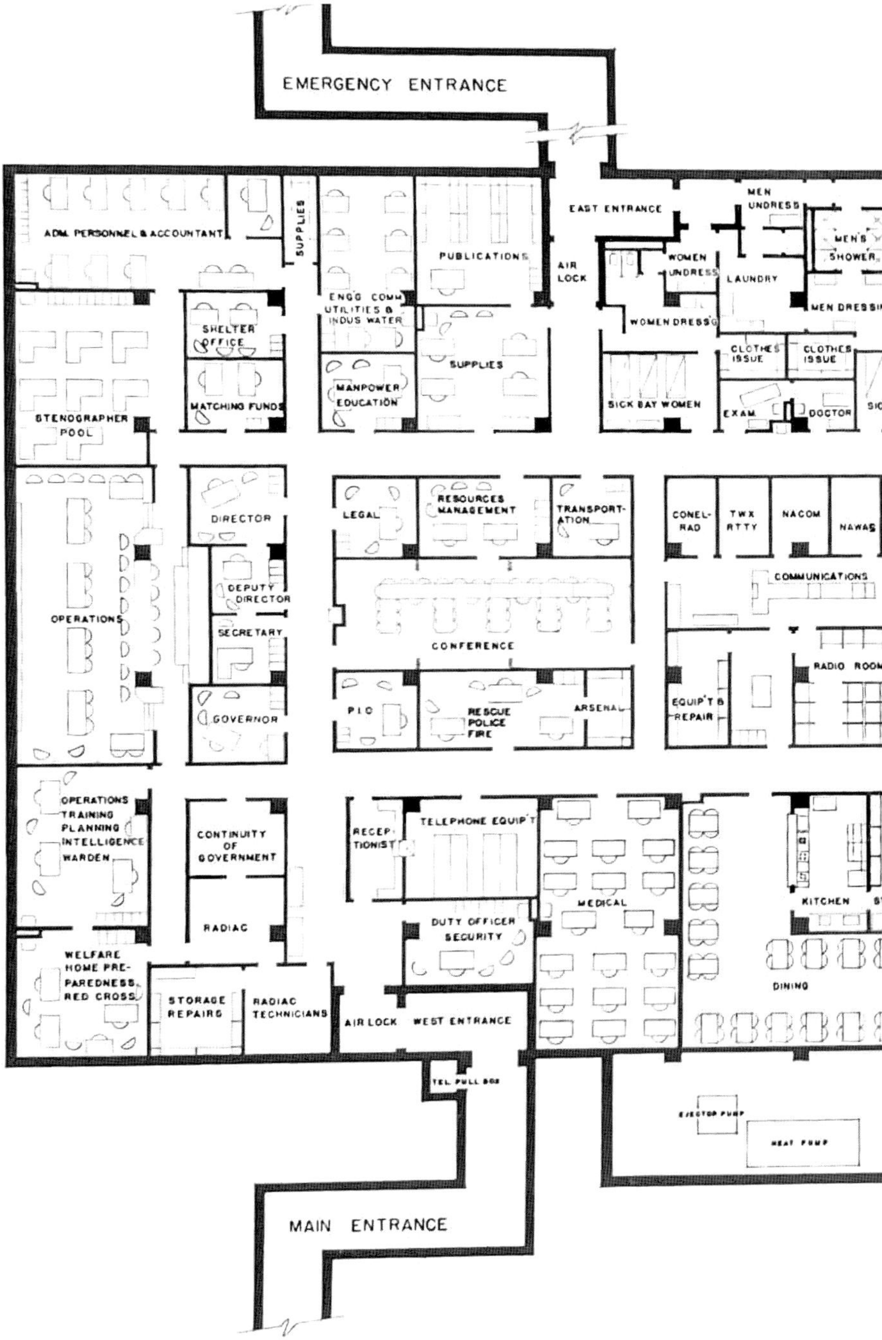
EMERGENCY ENTRANCE
ADM. PERSONNEL & ACCOUNTANT
SUPPLIES
PUBLICATIONS
EAST ENTRANCE
AIR LOCK
MEN UNDRESS
MEN'S SHOWER
WOMEN UNDRESS
LAUNDRY
MEN DRESSING
WOMEN DRESS'G
SHELTER OFFICE
ENG'G COMM UTILITIES & INDUS WATER
SUPPLIES
CLOTHES ISSUE
CLOTHES ISSUE
MATCHING FUNDS
MANPOWER EDUCATION
SICK BAY WOMEN
EXAM
DOCTOR
STENOGRAPHER POOL
DIRECTOR
LEGAL
RESOURCES MANAGEMENT
TRANSPORTATION
CONEL-RAD
TWX RTTY
NACOM
NAWAS
DEPUTY DIRECTOR
COMMUNICATIONS
OPERATIONS
SECRETARY
CONFERENCE
RADIO ROOM
GOVERNOR
PIO
RESCUE POLICE FIRE
ARSENAL
EQUIP'T & REPAIR
OPERATIONS TRAINING PLANNING INTELLIGENCE WARDEN
CONTINUITY OF GOVERNMENT
RECEPTIONIST
TELEPHONE EQUIP'T
MEDICAL
KITCHEN
RADIAC
DUTY OFFICER SECURITY
WELFARE HOME PREPAREDNESS RED CROSS
DINING
STORAGE REPAIRS
RADIAC TECHNICIANS
AIR LOCK
WEST ENTRANCE
TEL PULL BOX
EJECTOR PUMP
HEAT PUMP
MAIN ENTRANCE

MASSACHUSETTS
CIVIL DEFENSE
EMERGENCY
OPERATING CENTER

S S EISENBERG A I A - ARCHITECTS

BOSTON, MASSACHUSETTS

Previous: The 1963 Massachusetts Civil Defense Emergency Operating Center floor plan shows the original layout, which has evolved over time to enhance emergency response capabilities. *MEMA*.

Left: In 1963, Massachusetts dedicated the nation's first Civil Defense Center in Framingham, a $3 million facility serving as the emergency communication hub and government headquarters in case of disaster. *MEMA*.

Below: Under construction in the early 1960s, Massachusetts was the first state to have an underground blast-proof State Emergency Operations Center, part of JFK's continuity plan. *MEMA*.

Massachusetts Civil Defense Agency staff managing critical operations inside the Framingham Bunker, 1969. This facility served as a command center for civil defense activities. *MEMA*.

designed as a public shelter but as a secure location for the governor and essential staff to manage state operations during a disaster. Its construction reflected the heightened emphasis on preparedness and resilience against both man-made and natural threats during the Cold War era.

The Bunker incorporated several unique features designed to withstand a nuclear blast and its aftermath. The facility's internal walls were primarily made of asbestos panels, a durable and fire-resistant material common in that era.

In recent years, significant renovations have modernized the Bunker while preserving its historical integrity. Upgrades included LED lighting, a solar array and a complete building sprinkler system to enhance safety and energy efficiency. Advanced audiovisual systems were installed to facilitate seamless communication during emergencies, and the operations room was adapted to serve multiple functions. The room could accommodate various emergency support functions, integrating modern technology for power, data and communication.

The Bunker's mechanical room, which houses original systems, was designed to ensure self-sufficiency. It is equipped with 240-foot wells for potable water, nonpotable water tanks for other uses, redundant power supplies from two separate feeds and multiple generators to ensure continuous operation during extended outages. The HVAC system was upgraded to modern standards, maintaining its original purpose of filtering and recirculating air within the Bunker. Additionally, a morgue was included as a necessary feature, reflecting the grim reality that some occupants might not survive a prolonged stay underground.

Communication has always been a crucial aspect of the Bunker's design. It houses an emergency broadcast system and maintains direct lines to state police and other critical agencies. The dispatch center is a vital hub for coordinating responses to various emergencies, equipped to handle national alerts and push out wireless emergency alerts when necessary.

Throughout its history, the Bunker has been used for various emergency management exercises and real events. It has evolved from its original Cold

The blast door at the entrance to the MEMA Emergency Operations Center is nine inches thick, weighs nearly three tons and was designed to withstand explosions. *MEMA*.

Left: Massachusetts Emergency Management Agency's challenge coin commemorates the sixtieth anniversary of the State Emergency Operations Center, "The Bunker," which opened on November 16, 1963. *MEMA.*

Below: Kenneth O'Donnell wrote to Daniel Finn, Civil Defense Agency director, on November 22, 1963, the day JFK was assassinated, regarding the state Emergency Operations Center. *MEMA.*

THE WHITE HOUSE
WASHINGTON

November 22, 1963

Dear Dan:

Although it was not possible to send a statement in connection with the dedication of the new Emergency Operating Center on November 16th, the President was happy to inscribe a photograph for the Center and it is being sent herewith.

With best wishes,

Sincerely,

Kenneth O'Donnell
Kenneth O'Donnell
Special Assistant to the President

Mr. Daniel J. Finn
Director
Civil Defense Agency
400 Worcester Road
Framingham, Massachusetts

War purpose to a modern emergency management facility, adapting to new challenges and technological advancements while maintaining its historical legacy. The Bunker's role in events such as the Boston Marathon showcases its importance as a central hub for coordinating large-scale emergency responses.

President John F. Kennedy's administration was pivotal in the creation of the Bunker. His vision to have such facilities in each state for emergency preparedness led to the construction of the Massachusetts Bunker, the first in the nation. Although JFK could not attend the dedication ceremony, he sent a letter that was read on his behalf, marking the significance of this initiative. Additionally, a separate bunker was built for JFK on Nantucket in 1962 by the Navy Seabees, unrelated to the Framingham Bunker.

Boston Civil Defense: Boston City Hall (1963)

David Monteyne, in his book *Fallout Shelter*, discusses the design and construction of Boston City Hall, completed between 1963 and 1968 by the architectural firm Kallmann, McKinnell & Knowles. Monteyne emphasizes how the building's "bunker aesthetic" was a product of its architectural features rather than an intentional design for civil defense. The building's exposed rough concrete, small and dark window openings, heavy cornices and deep overhangs create a fortress-like appearance. Despite not being initially designed as a fallout shelter, these elements provided substantial fallout protection due to their inherent characteristics.

Boston City Hall's massive concrete structure and partially below–ground level positioning enhanced its protective quality. The expansive plaza surrounding the building further accentuated its imposing presence. Although the architects did not explicitly design the building for civil defense, it inherently offered significant fallout protection, which was later recognized and utilized.

An Emergency Operations Center (EOC) was incorporated into the building soon after its initial construction using federal matching funds. Located two floors below the plaza level and shielded by thick concrete walls, the EOC was essentially a bunker. It was equipped to support fifty personnel, including the mayor and department heads, for up to two weeks. The EOC featured cooking and dining facilities, a cistern and a bank of radios for communication with essential city departments. Closed-circuit television cameras provided real-time visuals of the plaza, essential for monitoring post-attack or protest situations.

Boston City Hall, a massive concrete structure, began construction in 1963. Initially not a fallout shelter, it was later equipped to protect almost twenty thousand citizens. *Boston Public Library*.

Monteyne notes that Boston City Hall was designated as a fallout shelter with the capacity to protect up to nineteen thousand people. The building stored various supplies, including water drums, boxes of biscuits, first aid kits, sanitation supplies and radiation monitoring equipment in its sub-basements. These supplies underscored the city's commitment to civil defense and aligned with broader national strategies during the Cold War. The public areas of Boston City Hall, such as the atrium and concourse on the second and third floors, were identified as potential shelter areas. These spaces were designed to inspire confidence in the continuity of democratic civilization during an attack, although the conditions would have been spartan, with citizens likely sleeping on hard floors due to the lack of cots.

Boston City Hall was later featured in Office of Civil Defense (OCD) publications, indicating that buildings not explicitly designed for fallout protection but possessing inherent protective qualities could serve as examples in civil defense promotion. This reflects the OCD's strategy of fostering a broader cultural association of architecture with protection, subtly influencing public building design trends during the Cold War.

Boston played a significant role in national civil defense initiatives, often serving as a testing ground for new emergency planning strategies. The Government Center urban renewal project exemplifies Boston's proactive approach. This project involved constructing new buildings for federal, state and city government offices, incorporating fallout protection into these structures. In 1951, Boston officials participated in a civil defense exercise simulating an attack on Scollay Square, a dilapidated area later chosen as the site for the new city hall. This exercise underscored Boston's commitment to refining its emergency response protocols.

The EOC's inclusion in Boston City Hall further solidified the building's role in civil defense. Although not part of the initial space planning, the EOC was a crucial addition. Equipped to support essential personnel for extended periods, it featured necessary facilities and communication tools, underscoring the building's capacity to function as a command center in emergencies. The design's unintentional fallout protection capabilities highlighted Boston's proactive approach to civil defense, positioning it as a model city for national fallout shelter programs.

Boston City Hall's substantial structure, concrete waffle slabs, overhangs and integration into the site's grade contributed to its fallout protection capabilities. These features, although not initially intended for civil defense, made the building effective in providing protection. Public perception and civil defense publications later reinforced this unintended role, showcasing how the building's design inadvertently aligned with Cold War–era civil defense strategies.

While Boston actively embraced civil defense measures, the effectiveness of such efforts, particularly in the face of a nuclear attack, was debated. Nonetheless, Boston's involvement in civil defense activities surpassed that of many other cities, demonstrating its commitment to preparedness and protection during the Cold War era. The building's design and the incorporation of the EOC highlight Boston's proactive stance, making it a prominent example of civil defense functionality blended with modernist architectural design.

Boston Common Garage

In the early 1950s, Boston officials proposed an innovative project to build a $12 million underground garage beneath Boston Common that would also function as a nuclear bomb shelter. This dual-purpose facility was designed to alleviate parking congestion while providing protection for up to fifty thousand people in the event of a nuclear attack, reflecting the Cold War era's civil defense concerns.

Mayor John B. Hynes and Governor Paul A. Dever strongly advocated for the project, securing support from President Truman and a substantial loan from the Reconstruction Finance Corporation (RFC), contingent on additional financial guarantees from Motor Parks Inc. The planned structure would feature three levels, robust enough to withstand a nuclear blast, with provisions for food, medical supplies and independent oxygen and ventilation systems, ensuring the safety of thousands for up to two weeks.

However, the project quickly became controversial. Representative Sherman Miles, a retired army general, criticized the plan as impractical and accused proponents of using the "bomb scare" to manipulate public sentiment and secure funding. Miles argued that the proposal was designed to scare people into supporting a project that private interests did not back. He also pointed out the logistical challenges of using a large garage as a bomb shelter, suggesting that smaller, localized shelters would be more effective in an emergency.

Financial and administrative challenges further delayed the project. The RFC loan required substantial securities and financial conditions that Motor Parks Inc. struggled to meet. These complications slowed progress and added to the controversy surrounding the feasibility and fiscal responsibility of the project.

By the late 1950s, the plans had been revised, and the emphasis on the bomb shelter aspect was diminished. Construction eventually proceeded with a primary focus on addressing Boston's parking needs. The Boston Common garage opened in November 1961, featuring three levels and accommodating 1,350 cars. While it incorporated some robust structural features, it did not fully realize the original vision of a combined bomb shelter.

The Boston Common garage project illustrates the complexities of urban planning during the Cold War, when civil defense concerns intersected with practical urban needs. Despite significant support and innovative planning, the project's controversial aspects and financial hurdles ultimately led to a scaled-back version that primarily served as a parking facility.

State House

In August 1961, a fallout shelter was opened for the governor and key state officials beneath the front lawn of the State House. Situated thirty feet underground, this shelter served as a safe space in emergencies, including nuclear attacks, and as headquarters for the State House Civil Defense organization. The shelter measured eighteen by ten feet and was located in the sub-basement of the new underground Archives Building. It could accommodate up to twelve people.

According to Capital Police Chief Paul Doherty, the shelter could endure a nuclear bomb and radioactive fallout. It was equipped with air conditioning, heating and independent lighting powered by separate generators. Plans included stocking the shelter with radio equipment, food, water and other necessary supplies for a two-week stay.

Boston Tunnels

In December 1961, William F. Callahan, the chairman of the Massachusetts Turnpike Authority, proposed using the Sumner and Callahan vehicular tunnels as public fallout shelters. He informed State Civil Defense Director John J. Maginnis that these tunnels could be adapted to shelter residents from the densely populated North End and East Boston areas. Additionally, Callahan noted that several buildings in East Boston and the North End could be used to store large supplies of food and essential materials in case of a nuclear attack.

First National Bank Boston at Pepperell (1960–1991)

The Underground Records Storage Center, initiated by the First National Bank of Boston in Pepperell, Massachusetts, represents a significant investment in disaster resilience and record preservation. Launched on December 1, 1960, the center was built at a total cost of $170,000, with approximately $24,000 allocated specifically for excavation and drilling, essential for its robust infrastructure.

Originally serving the First National Bank of Boston and several other prominent New England banks, the facility's role evolved over the decades. By 1991, it had transitioned to the ownership of Archive Storage Inc., catering to the storage needs of various media essential for business operations, from computer magnetic tapes to microfilms.

Constructed to endure the impact of any known explosives within a five-mile radius, the vault's structure features walls and a floor made from about 1,500 cubic yards of concrete and reinforced with roughly 100 tons of steel. It includes various emergency support systems, such as a gasoline-powered generator, an internal well extending 426 feet below ground for water supply and advanced air filtration and conditioning systems to protect against radiation and other contaminants.

The bunker was equipped with sophisticated climate control and safety systems to ensure the optimal preservation of sensitive materials. The climate control system maintained the temperature within a consistent range of forty-five to sixty degrees Fahrenheit, with a constant humidity level between 45 and 55 percent, which was crucial for preventing damage to computer media and other delicate records. Additionally, the facility boasted a Halon fire suppression system, which could quickly extinguish fires without harming the stored media. This system was essential for protecting valuable data from fire damage, a common risk in storage facilities. To safeguard against seismic activity, the infrastructure included seismic hangers suspending the system's piping from the ceiling, ensuring that even in the event of an earthquake, the structural integrity of the fire suppression setup would remain uncompromised. All the facility's wiring was encased in concrete, providing further protection against both seismic events and fire.

Security at the center was stringent, guarded by an eight-ton vault door, which originally served as a bank vault door, and a unique U.S. Navy surplus escape hatch labeled "USS Nautilus" for an additional secure exit. Designed not just as a records storage facility but also as a crisis bunker for top executives during emergencies, it featured comprehensive survival provisions.

The facility was equipped with twenty-four-hour armed guards, machine guns, protective clothing and enough food supplies—calculated at 842 calories per person per day—to last for two weeks. The self-sustaining features also included its own water supply from an underground well, ensuring a fully operational and isolated environment.

This dual-purpose facility served as both a safeguard for financial records and an emergency shelter, highlighting its critical role in ensuring operational continuity and the well-being of its occupants during extended periods of isolation or external threats during the Cold War era.

This historical facility not only highlights the Cold War's influence on infrastructural development but also emphasizes the enduring importance of data preservation and security. Modern data centers, while more technologically advanced, continue to employ the foundational principles of disaster resilience, stringent security and environmental control demonstrated by the Pepperell facility. This legacy underscores the ongoing challenge of safeguarding critical information in an era when data is both an invaluable asset and a potential liability.

Clinton Tunnel

In December 1961, the Clinton Tunnel, an abandoned railroad tunnel, was converted into a community fallout shelter as part of Massachusetts's civil defense initiatives. An open house event was organized, allowing citizens to tour the newly repurposed facility and learn about its use in case of a nuclear threat.

Hoosac Tunnel

On October 25, 1962, in North Berkshire, the Hoosac Tunnel was identified as a massive fallout shelter capable of protecting 31,300 people, which matched the population of North Adams and Adams. According to a civil defense report prepared by the U.S. Army engineers, the tunnel was 65,200 square feet and could accommodate 15,650,000 cubic feet. The tunnel, built in 1874, was located under the Hoosac Mountain range.

Hancock Bunker

Andre Rambaud dedicated his life to developing robust infrastructure for emergency preparedness in Hancock, Massachusetts. Serving as the civil defense director for forty years, Rambaud played a crucial role in ensuring the safety of his community. His journey began in 1960, when he moved to the scenic Berkshire County to escape the suburban sprawl of Long Island. Settling in Hancock, Rambaud purchased his first two hundred acres in 1960, expanding to a total of three hundred acres by 1965, and he established the Privacy Campground in 1969.

Rambaud's interest in civil defense and emergency preparedness grew from his early experiences as a child escaping Nazi-occupied France and his later military service during the Korean War. His fascination with building bomb shelters was sparked during World War II and further fueled by the Cold War. In the late 1970s, he began constructing a large family bunker and a public shelter on his property. His efforts were a response to the growing concerns of nuclear threats and other disasters.

The family bunker, completed with the help of his wife, Birgit, and daughter Veronica, was built into the side of a hill, featuring walls made of soil and concrete, with recycled elevator doors for added protection. This smaller shelter, located under their winter home, included a wood stove for heating and a water recycling system and was designed to accommodate three people in cramped conditions.

In contrast, the public shelter was a more extensive structure. Measuring sixty by twenty-five feet with twelve-inch-thick walls, it could house up to one hundred people. Rambaud equipped this shelter with recycled doors, sink stalls and a wood stove for heating. He planned to install a periscope for outside viewing and utilized various sources for electricity, including a commercial electrical system, windmill and gasoline-powered generators.

Rambaud's ingenuity extended to the hydroelectric system he developed to power his campground. He created a reservoir fed by a mountain aquifer, which piped water down to a turbine in the public shelter, generating sufficient power to meet the campground's needs. His property also hosted wind turbines as part of the Berkshire Wind Power Cooperative.

Throughout the years, Rambaud continued to enhance his emergency preparedness measures. His personal bunker featured a 1,700-pound door, gas masks, a Geiger counter and an elaborate security system. He even built an eighty-two-foot tunnel connecting the personal and public shelters, allowing for quick access in times of need.

Metropolitan Water Works

During the Cold War, Massachusetts faced considerable challenges in managing its drinking water infrastructure amid the pervasive nuclear threat. This era was characterized by intense geopolitical tension and the looming possibility of nuclear warfare, which prompted state and local governments to implement stringent measures to ensure public safety, particularly in water supply management.

The Cold War commenced with the detonation of atomic bombs at the end of World War II, igniting a nuclear arms race that heightened global apprehensions. In Massachusetts, this concern was particularly acute due to its dense population and industrial significance. Water suppliers in urban centers like Boston received detailed briefings on the potential impacts of nuclear strikes, including projected casualty figures and the extent of expected infrastructural damage. These briefings were essential, shaping emergency preparedness and response strategies within the water supply sector.

The period was also marked by extensive nuclear testing, particularly by the United States and the Soviet Union, leading to widespread radioactive fallout. This fallout contaminated surface waters globally, including in New England, where it raised significant public health concerns. The detection of radioactivity in local water sources spurred advancements in monitoring technologies and methodologies, enhancing the capacity to assess environmental contamination and manage associated risks more effectively.

Research played a pivotal role in Massachusetts's response to these threats. From 1952 to 1955, a collaborative effort between Harvard University and the U.S. Atomic Energy Commission involved extensive monitoring of rain and stream water samples throughout eastern Massachusetts. This initiative aimed to quantify the extent of radioactive contamination from nuclear testing and its impact on water supplies. The findings underscored the presence of radioactive materials in the water, reinforcing the need for ongoing vigilance and improvements in water treatment processes to mitigate potential health hazards

Springfield, Massachusetts, exemplified the local challenges and adaptive strategies necessitated by the Cold War. A 1963 Federal Office of Civil Defense report identified specific vulnerabilities of Springfield's water system to radioactive fallout, notably at exposed-surface reservoirs such as Cobble Mountain Reservoir and Bordon Brook Reservoir. Despite these vulnerabilities, Springfield's water infrastructure included several protective features, such as covered reservoirs and a gravity-fed distribution system, which minimized reliance on electrical power and enhanced the system's resilience against disruptions.

Additional protective measures were implemented to ensure the safety of operational personnel. Infrastructure enhancements at key facilities provided improved radiation shielding and emergency capabilities, enabling essential staff to continue operations safely during fallout conditions. Springfield also maintained substantial covered water storage, capable of supporting the city for up to sixteen months on restricted usage, highlighting its preparedness for extended emergency scenarios.

Throughout the Cold War, the imperative for adaptability and foresight in public utility management was starkly evident. Massachusetts actively pursued research into more effective water treatment techniques and emergency management strategies, aiming to fortify its water systems against the impacts of radioactive fallout. This proactive approach in Springfield and across the state demonstrated a strong commitment to maintaining safe, reliable drinking water supplies in the face of unprecedented nuclear threats, reflecting broader concerns during the era about nuclear preparedness and the need for robust civil defense infrastructure.

COLD WAR CHALLENGES AND ADAPTATIONS

Contemporary Warning and Emergency Communication Systems

AT&T Microwave Between Boston and New York City

In 1947, as tensions heightened during the Cold War, the United States government implemented various civil defense measures to prepare for the possibility of a nuclear attack. Central to these efforts was the development and evolution of emergency communication and public protection systems. This narrative chronicles the progression of these initiatives from the mid-1950s to the early 1960s, highlighting key developments and technological advancements.

The CONELRAD (Control of Electromagnetic Radiation) system was established in 1951 under an executive order by President Truman. It was designed to confuse enemy planes and missiles by using commercial radio beams. The system relied on two specific frequencies, 640 and 1240 kHz, to broadcast emergency information during an attack.

On July 20, 1956, the nation participated in a CONELRAD drill, marking a significant effort in civil defense preparedness. From 4:10 to 4:25 p.m., all radio and television stations went off the air. Certain authorized stations then broadcasted on the designated frequencies meant for civil defense communications. This drill aimed to familiarize the public with the

CONELRAD system, which would be critical in disseminating information during a real threat. In Boston, stations like WBZ, WNAC, WEEI and WHDH participated, but listeners reported mixed experiences. The reception was often inconsistent, with signals fading in and out, making it difficult to follow the broadcasts due to interference and noise. Despite these issues, the exercise was a crucial step in testing the nation's readiness and the effectiveness of CONELRAD.

Three years later, on April 10, 1959, Operation Alert exercises across the nation had a significant focus in Massachusetts. This exercise simulated five bomb bursts and one dud to test the state's preparedness for a nuclear attack. The operation involved over ten thousand civil defense workers, who mapped fallout patterns and assessed the fallout's intensity. The test aimed to evaluate the state's ability to survive and respond effectively, revealing strengths in advanced medical services and comprehensive training programs while also highlighting areas needing improvement, particularly in public awareness and shelter preparedness.

In September 1960, further advancements in emergency alert systems were announced. Civil defense officials introduced the National Emergency Alarm Repeater (NEAR), a small buzzer device designed to provide almost instantaneous warning of an enemy attack. The buzzer, which could be plugged into any household electrical outlet, emitted a continuous, high-frequency sound loud enough to awaken people from deep sleep. Activated by sending a special electrical signal through existing power lines, the system allowed for a nationwide alert in approximately one minute. The first large-scale demonstration of NEAR was scheduled for October 1, when it would be installed in two thousand homes, schools, factories, government facilities and businesses. This system, developed after a year of research and a $90,000 investment, was designed to avoid false alarms and not interfere with normal electrical usage.

By November 1961, plans for the widespread implementation of NEAR in over fifty million homes were progressing. The system aimed to install buzzers in households across the United States, providing a loud, high-frequency alert to prompt residents to tune into the CONELRAD frequencies for further instructions during an emergency. Initially, a large-scale test was planned but later deemed unnecessary due to sufficient development and smaller tests proving the system's effectiveness. The NEAR system, expected to cost up to $1 billion nationwide, would be funded initially by the federal government for installation in utility systems, with individual homeowners possibly repaying the cost of their alarm units.

An army H-21 Helicopter transports a HELICOP-HUT Air Traffic Control Set during Operation Alert in Danvers, 1954. This mobile tower sets up in thirty minutes. *Digital Commonwealth.*

In December 1961, a significant contract was awarded to a Boston firm for the construction of fallout shelters in New England as part of the national civil defense program. This effort aimed to provide shelters with a minimum protection factor of 80 percent, reducing radiation exposure by at least 80 percent. The initial phase of the program included utilizing existing federal buildings and incorporating fallout shelters into new federal structures. Approximately $17.5 million was allocated for this effort, with $10 million dedicated to improving existing buildings to protect 250,000 people and $7.5 million for planning shelters for 680,000 people in new buildings. Additionally, plans were developed to equip 1,300 CONELRAD stations with standby power and radio links to local or regional civil defense headquarters.

Massachusetts was set to receive nineteen contracts, with more across New England. Each shelter was expected to protect at least fifty people, and public information programs would guide residents on locating and using these shelters. State officials also explored converting tunnels, caves and other structures into fallout shelters. The chairman of the Massachusetts Turnpike Authority proposed using the Sumner and Callahan Tunnels as shelters for residents of densely populated areas, emphasizing the feasibility of adapting these structures for public protection. In Worcester County, the abandoned rail tunnel in Clinton was considered for use as a fallout shelter, as was the Hoosac Tunnel, which was estimated to have a capacity of more than thirty thousand people. This comprehensive plan aimed to maximize the use of existing resources and infrastructure to protect the populace in the event of a nuclear threat.

In parallel with these efforts, the development of a robust telecommunications system was underway. During the late 1950s, the U.S. federal government recognized the importance of a unified telecommunications network capable of handling both daily administrative needs and emergency communications for all civilian agencies. This led to the formulation of plans for the Federal Telecommunications System (FTS), a dedicated network providing reliable and survivable communications. Early in 1961, the General Services Administration (GSA) received authorization to implement FTS, spurred by events like the Cuban Missile Crisis, which had highlighted the inadequacies of the government's reliance on public communication services.

In March 1962, the Bell System committed to establishing Phase I of FTS, and by February 15, 1963, the first phase was officially launched, serving 42 cities, including Boston. Each center featured a major switching machine, connecting the centers via final trunks. As Phase I was being implemented, plans for Phase II were already in motion, aiming to expand the network to serve eight thousand government locations in 350 cities.

By July 1963, it was clear that CONELRAD had become obsolete. Although it was originally designed to confuse enemy planes and missiles, advancements in navigation technology had rendered the system ineffective. The new Emergency Broadcast System (EBS) was set to replace it, utilizing the entire AM broadcast band and allowing authorized stations to remain on their usual frequencies during an emergency. Under EBS, stations would identify themselves geographically but not by call letters, ensuring that all stations in a specified area would broadcast the same material from a single source. This changeover was expected to occur on August 5, 1963, marking a significant improvement in the nation's emergency communication capabilities.

The evolution of civil defense measures in the United States during the Cold War era demonstrates the government's commitment to protecting

Westfield's civil defense director and deputy operate a new card dial telephone in 1963. This innovation boosted speed and reduced call errors. *MCDA.*

its citizens from potential nuclear threats. From the initial implementation of CONELRAD to the development of NEAR and the eventual transition to EBS and the establishment of the FTS, these efforts highlight the continuous advancements in technology and strategy aimed at ensuring public safety in times of crisis. The construction of fallout shelters and the establishment of comprehensive communication systems were critical components of the nation's preparedness, reflecting a proactive approach to civil defense during one of the most tense periods in modern history. These initiatives show how the U.S. government adapted to the growing threats of the Cold War by developing sophisticated systems for emergency communications and public protection.

Research and Engineering

The Cold War era was marked by rapid advancements in technology and defense systems, particularly in the United States, which sought to counter the growing threat from the Soviet Union. Central to these efforts were several key organizations and projects, many based in Massachusetts. The development and implementation of these technologies not only revolutionized air defense but also established lasting relationships among prominent institutions like MIT, Lincoln Laboratory, MITRE, Draper Labs and Raytheon.

In the early 1950s, as Cold War tensions escalated, the United States Air Force (USAF) contracted the Massachusetts Institute of Technology to create Lincoln Laboratory. This research facility was dedicated to advancing air defense capabilities, resulting in the development of the Semi-Automated Ground Environment system. Initiated in 1951, the SAGE system was a revolutionary advancement in air defense, leveraging cutting-edge computer technology to detect and intercept enemy aircraft.

By 1958, MIT's concern about producing operational systems led to the creation of MITRE. The USAF spun off the Digital Computer Division of Lincoln Laboratory to form MITRE, which took over SAGE system engineering. On January 1, 1959, 485 employees from Lincoln Laboratory transferred to MITRE, ensuring the continuity and technical competence of the SAGE project. Although MIT and Lincoln Laboratory were no longer officially connected to MITRE, the collaboration highlighted the seamless transition from research to operational implementation.

Raytheon, based in Massachusetts, played a pivotal role in the defense and technology sectors during the Cold War. Founded in 1922 near MIT, the company initially focused on radio tubes but quickly expanded its technological capabilities. During World War II, Raytheon's development of the magnetron was critical for radar technology, which was vital for the Allies' success. This innovation laid the groundwork for Raytheon's postwar expansion into missile systems and other defense technologies.

In the Cold War era, Raytheon's work on radar and missile systems was crucial. The company developed the guided Lark missile in the late 1940s, which made a historic intercept of a drone target in flight. Additionally, Raytheon was involved in early-warning systems, contributing to the development of phased array radars during the 1950s and 1960s. These radars were essential for the U.S. military's early detection capabilities, helping maintain strategic advantages during the tense geopolitical climate of the Cold War.

Raytheon's relationships with government agencies and other laboratories were significant throughout the Cold War. The company collaborated closely with the U.S. military, providing advanced technology and systems that were integral to national defense.

Raytheon's role extended to the development of the Distant Early Warning Line, specifically their involvement in producing automatic alerting radar. The DEW Line installations in the Arctic faced staffing challenges, necessitating automatic alerting radars to minimize the number of technicians at each site. Raytheon's involvement began after successful prototyping at Lincoln Laboratory, taking on the production of the final design, which was deployed along the DEW Line.

A recurring theme in the development of the SAGE system and related projects was Lincoln Laboratory's pioneering role in research and development. They led the prototyping of new technologies, such as the automatic alerting radar, and once proven effective, these technologies were transitioned to industrial partners like Raytheon for large-scale production and deployment. This approach ensured a robust and efficient development cycle for critical national security technologies.

One of Raytheon's notable projects during this period was the development of the Patriot Air and Missile Defense System in the 1980s, which became one of the world's most renowned defense systems.

By the end of the Cold War, Raytheon had established itself as a leader in defense and aerospace technology, with a strong foundation in Massachusetts and a broad impact on global defense strategies.

Naval Weapons Industrial Reserve Plant at Bedford (1952)

In 1952, the Naval Weapons Industrial Reserve Plant (NWIRP) Bedford was established in Bedford, Massachusetts, as a government-owned, contractor-operated facility. Initially overseen by the U.S. Naval Air Systems Command (NAVAIR) and operated by the Raytheon Manufacturing Company, the facility later came under the management of the U.S. Naval Sea Systems Command (NAVSEA). Covering forty-six acres, NWIRP Bedford played a crucial role in developing radar and missile guidance systems during the Cold War, with Raytheon leading efforts on significant missile systems like the Hawk, Sparrow III, SAM-D and Patriot missiles.

The creation of NWIRP Bedford was part of a broader strategy where the U.S. government retained ownership of industrial plants while private companies managed their day-to-day operations. This model, known as the government-owned, contractor-operated (GOCO) system, emerged during World War II and continued through the Cold War to ensure readiness and support for defense production. The facility supported Raytheon's research and development of radar and missile guidance systems, starting with the Lark missile program in the late 1940s, which helped establish Bedford as a center for missile technology.

One of the early successes at NWIRP Bedford was the development of the Sparrow III missile in the early 1950s. This radar-guided, air-to-air missile underwent several improvements over the years, becoming a staple in the U.S. military's arsenal and widely used by NATO forces. Another significant project was the Hawk missile, which Raytheon began developing in 1954. The Hawk surface-to-air missile provided medium-range air defense and, although never used in combat by U.S. forces, was continuously upgraded and remained in service for several decades. The Patriot missile, which started as the SAM-D program in the 1960s, was another major achievement. By the 1980s, the Patriot system was operational and gained prominence during the Gulf War for its defense against Iraqi Scud missiles.

As NWIRP Bedford's operations expanded, so did its facilities. The site included specialized buildings such as the Components Laboratory, Flight Test Facility and the Antenna Range Building, which supported the design, testing and development of advanced missile systems and radar technologies. Over the years, NWIRP Bedford continued to grow, adding new buildings and upgrading existing ones to accommodate the increasing scope of research and development activities.

However, by the late 1990s, changes in defense strategies and the end of the Cold War led to a reduced need for such extensive GOCO facilities. In 2000, Raytheon ceased operations at NWIRP Bedford, and the U.S. Navy declared the property excess. The site was largely cleared and vacated, marking the end of an era for this key player in the nation's defense infrastructure.

Despite its closure, the legacy of NWIRP Bedford endures. The site played a pivotal role during the Cold War, contributing to significant advancements in missile technology and radar systems. Its historical significance is recognized through its eligibility for listing in the National Register of Historic Places, ensuring that the contributions of NWIRP Bedford to national defense are remembered and honored.

Draper Laboratory

Draper Labs, originally known as the MIT Instrumentation Laboratory, played a pivotal role in the United States' efforts to maintain strategic superiority during the Cold War. Founded by Dr. Charles Stark Draper in 1932 and headquartered in Cambridge, Massachusetts, Draper Labs specialized in precision instrumentation and control systems. Throughout the Cold War, the lab was instrumental in developing guidance systems for missiles, working in close collaboration with MIT, Lincoln Labs, the U.S. Navy, the U.S. Air Force and other defense entities. While Draper Labs conducted most of its research and development in and around Cambridge, Massachusetts, the testing and deployment of these systems took place at various locations across the United States.

Draper Labs' journey began with foundational work in precision instrumentation, laying the groundwork for its future contributions to missile guidance systems. In the late 1950s, Draper Labs embarked on the development of the guidance system for the UGM-27 Polaris, a submarine-launched ballistic missile. This project, initiated by the U.S. Navy in 1956, aimed to establish a reliable deterrent force that could be deployed from submarines. Draper Labs designed an inertial guidance system that allowed Polaris missiles to be launched from underwater and strike distant targets with high precision, significantly enhancing the U.S. Navy's strategic nuclear capabilities and maintaining a credible deterrent against Soviet aggression. The Polaris missile entered service in 1960.

Following the success of the Polaris program, Draper Labs continued to develop guidance systems for the next generation of SLBMs. From the late 1960s through the 1980s, the lab played a crucial role in the Poseidon missile, which featured greater payload capacity and improved accuracy. Subsequently, Draper Labs worked on the Trident missile systems. These Trident missiles, known for their long range and pinpoint accuracy, became the backbone of the U.S. Navy's strategic deterrence force. The guidance systems developed by Draper Labs ensured that these missiles could reliably deliver their warheads to targets thousands of miles away, thereby bolstering the United States' second-strike capability. The Poseidon missile entered service in 1971 and the Trident I in 1979, followed by the Trident II in 1990.

During this period, Draper Labs extensively collaborated with Lincoln Laboratory, another MIT-affiliated institution established in 1951 to address the nation's urgent need for improved air defense systems in response to the Soviet threat. Lincoln Labs initially focused on radar technology, which complemented Draper Labs' expertise in guidance and control systems. Together, Draper Labs and Lincoln Labs made significant advancements in missile defense systems. Lincoln Labs' radar technology was crucial for identifying and tracking incoming threats, while Draper Labs' guidance systems enabled the precise navigation and control of interceptor missiles. This collaboration was evident in projects like the Nike antiaircraft missile system, where Lincoln Labs provided radar technology and Draper Labs developed the guidance system, ensuring accurate interception. The Nike project spanned from the early 1950s to the late 1960s.

Draper Labs also played a critical role in the Minuteman intercontinental ballistic missile (ICBM) program, which began in 1958 and became a key component of the United States' nuclear triad. Deployed in underground silos starting in the early 1960s, Minuteman missiles required highly reliable and accurate guidance systems. Draper Labs developed inertial guidance technology that provided the Minuteman ICBMs with exceptional accuracy.

In addition to working with the navy, Draper Labs collaborated with the U.S. Air Force on several missile projects. The work on the Thor Intermediate Range Ballistic Missile (IRBM) began in the mid-1950s. The Thor missile, deployed in Europe in 1959, and the Titan I and II missile programs benefited from Draper Labs' guidance systems. The Titan missiles, which served both as ICBMs and launch vehicles for the Gemini space missions, relied on Draper Labs' expertise to achieve their mission objectives. Titan I was deployed from 1962 to 1965 and Titan II from 1963 to 1987. The guidance system development occurred in Cambridge, while missile testing and launches took place at locations such as Cape Canaveral Air Force Station in Florida and Edwards Air Force Base in California.

During the 1980s, Draper Labs participated in development of the Peacekeeper/MX missile program. Capable of delivering up to ten warheads with precision, this system was operational by 1988.

Throughout the Cold War, Draper Labs pioneered several technological innovations in missile guidance. Their inertial guidance systems, using gyroscopes and accelerometers to navigate without external references, were particularly significant. These systems ensured that missiles could accurately reach their targets even in the absence of GPS or other navigational aids. Additionally, Draper Labs' work on digital computing and software development for guidance systems laid the groundwork for future advancements in aerospace and defense technologies.

Draper Labs' contributions during the Cold War were crucial in maintaining the United States' strategic edge over the Soviet Union. The

The Millstone Hill radar, built by Lincoln Laboratory in Westford, observed Sputnik I, the world's first artificial satellite, launched by the Soviet Union on October 4, 1957. *Digital Commonwealth.*

lab's work on missile guidance systems not only bolstered national defense but also influenced a wide range of technological developments. The precision and reliability of the systems developed by Draper Labs ensured that the United States could effectively deter Soviet threats, thereby playing a significant role in the broader context of Cold War geopolitics.

The partnership between Draper Labs and Lincoln Labs, along with collaborations with the U.S. Navy, Air Force and other defense entities, exemplified the power of interdisciplinary cooperation in achieving technological superiority.

Today, still headquartered in Cambridge and with facilities and campuses around Massachusetts and across the country, Draper Labs continues to be a leading research institution. Building on its legacy of innovation and collaboration, Draper addresses contemporary challenges in defense and aerospace. The lab's ongoing projects involve cutting-edge technologies in areas such as autonomous systems, precision navigation, cybersecurity and biomedical engineering. By maintaining strong partnerships with government agencies, industry leaders and academic institutions, Draper Labs remains at the forefront of developing solutions that enhance national security and advance technological frontiers.

Natick Labs

The Natick Research and Development Laboratories, located in Natick, Massachusetts, is a significant U.S. Army facility dedicated to researching and developing clothing, personal equipment and food systems for individual combat soldiers. Established in 1953, it consolidated activities that had previously been scattered across various locations during World War II. The complex is situated on the shore of Lake Cochituate and spans seventy-eight acres with fifty-six buildings.

The need for a centralized research facility became evident during World War II, as quartermaster research was spread out nationwide. In 1949, Congress authorized $11 million for a new laboratory, largely influenced by the Massachusetts Congressional Group led by John W. McCormack. Construction began in November 1952, and by October 1953, the facility was operational. It was unique for combining studies of human reactions to various environments with military equipment testing under different climatic conditions.

In the early 1960s, the laboratory's mission expanded. The Environmental Research Facilities from Fort Knox and the Food and Container Institute from Chicago were relocated to Natick. The facility was redesignated as the Natick Research and Development Laboratories in 1963. By 1967, the Navy Clothing and Textile Research Unit had also moved to Natick.

One of the most notable facilities at Natick is the Climatic Chambers Building, which includes arctic and tropic test chambers for environmental testing. This building can simulate a wide range of temperatures and conditions, helping measure the performance of clothing and equipment, as well as human responses.

The Natick Laboratories continue to be a central part of the U.S. Army's research and development efforts, contributing to advancements in military technology and equipment

The facility has also been involved in various food and material advancements. During John Glenn's 1962 space orbit, his meals were prepared at Natick's food lab, a precursor to modern space food. The lab contributed to the development of Spam, M&Ms and freeze-dried coffee. Additionally, early prototypes of bulletproof vests and the process for restructuring meat, important in food manufacturing today, were researched here.

Natick's influence extends to everyday items like energy bars and weather-resistant clothing, with Gore-Tex being a notable example. The lab's experimental work even included the creation of indestructible sandwiches and military shelters deployable via parachute.

Watertown Arsenal

The Watertown Arsenal, established in 1816, served primarily for the storage, repair and issue of military ordnance and later became a significant center for materials testing and metals research, contributing major technological advancements until its closure in 1967.

Building No. 100, known as the Horace Hardy Lester Reactor, represents a significant chapter in the history of U.S. Army materials research. The reactor was designed by the Army Materials Research Agency. Constructed in 1960 at a cost of approximately $1,300,000, it was operational until it was shut down in 1970.

The reactor was primarily used to study the effects of nuclear radiation on materials. Its nuclear radiation was used to examine how materials changed when radiation passed through them and how radiation affected the properties of materials.

Building No. 100 was the first nuclear reactor designed to meet the specific needs of U.S. Army materials research programs. The reactor's design was unique for its time, allowing multiple discrete experiments to be conducted simultaneously, a feature that was particularly valuable for the extensive materials testing at Watertown Arsenal. This facility continued the Arsenal's legacy of pioneering nondestructive materials testing methods, including the use of radiography for materials inspection, which began as early as 1922.

Architecturally, the reactor containment building is a cylindrical, tank-type structure with an elliptical domed top. The building measures eighty feet in diameter and stands approximately sixty-nine feet high, with a significant portion of its foundation extending below ground. The reactor's core was a water-cooled and moderated neutron reactor designed for ferrous-based materials research. When operational, it utilized aluminum uranium 235 alloy fuel elements and was capable of producing power initially at one megawatt, later increased to five megawatts in 1968.

Throughout its operational years, the reactor saw several modifications aimed at improving its capabilities and resolving operational issues, such as water leakage through the concrete biological shield. Notable upgrades included the installation of a cooling tower in 1965 and enhancements to the monitoring and alarm systems.

The significance of the Horace Hardy Lester Reactor extends beyond its architectural and technical features. It symbolizes a critical period in the history of the Watertown Arsenal, marking the last major phase of research development before the Arsenal's closure in 1967 and the sale of its eastern half in 1968. The reactor facilitated advanced materials testing that was foundational for numerous army programs and contributed to significant advancements in nondestructive testing methods.

The Horace Hardy Lester Reactor differed from more common reactor plants of the period because, instead of harnessing the heat produced for power generation, the nuclear radiation itself was the important product for their research applications. The Watertown Arsenal reactor was used to learn what the nuclear radiation revealed about materials as they passed through samples and how they affected or changed materials. The reactor was the only facility of its type operated by the U.S. Army. Operated by the U.S. Army Materials and Research Agency (AMRA) and licensed by the Atomic Energy Commission, the reactor enabled new areas of nondestructive materials testing and laboratory research for all army programs.

Anthrax Research at UMass–Amherst (1960s–89)

The University of Massachusetts has been deeply involved in controversial anthrax research, primarily focused on developing a vaccine for the lethal germ warfare agent. The research, which began in earnest in the 1980s, has seen multiple phases and significant scrutiny both from the scientific community and the public.

In the late 1980s, UMass's research included efforts to genetically engineer anthrax, aiming to create more effective vaccines. This work included transferring genes from different anthrax strains to better understand the mechanisms of the disease and develop countermeasures against it. The research budget was substantial, with reported federal grants totaling millions, underscoring the project's scale and significance.

Despite the scientific advancements, the research faced ethical and safety concerns. Public debates highlighted fears of biowarfare potential and the moral implications of such research. In meetings and public hearings, activists and community members expressed strong opposition to the research, questioning its necessity and potential misuse in military applications.

The controversy peaked when local health boards and community groups began to demand transparency and stricter adherence to safety and ethical standards. The debates often centered on the need for improved regulatory frameworks to ensure that such research did not inadvertently increase the risks associated with anthrax, both as a natural disease and as a potential bioweapon.

Ultimately, the research at UMass was halted. Key figures involved in the research admitted that although their work was aimed at vaccine development and not weapon creation, the surrounding controversies and the potential for misuse led to a reassessment of priorities. The end of the research marked a significant moment in the ongoing debate over the role of academic institutions in military-funded biological research.

Massachusetts's Role in Shaping National Security Policies

Electronics Research Center

In the early 1960s, the United States was deeply involved in the space race with the Soviet Union, marked by the Soviet Union's successful launch of Sputnik in 1957. This prompted the establishment of NASA in 1958 to advance America's space exploration capabilities. By May 1961, President John F. Kennedy had set an ambitious goal to land a man on the moon by the end of the decade, necessitating significant enhancements in NASA's technological and research capacities. This led to the proposal of establishing the Electronics Research Center (ERC) in Kendall Square, Cambridge, Massachusetts.

NASA began planning the ERC in the summer of 1963, intending it to become a premier facility for advancing the agency's electronics expertise. The decision was influenced by Boston's unique academic and industrial environment, particularly its proximity to the Massachusetts Institute of Technology and Harvard University. The site selection process, which involved evaluating eighty-nine potential locations, eventually focused on a twenty-nine-acre tract in Kendall Square, driven by the area's rich technological and academic resources.

The United States Army Corps of Engineers played a crucial role in the planning and construction phases of the ERC. Preconstruction planning commenced in 1963, with the USACE conducting extensive site studies. Initially, the studies included 89 suggested locations, but the list expanded to 160 as the USACE delved deeper into site feasibility, eventually homing in on Kendall Square. The USACE was responsible for clearing the site, which involved relocating ninety-four small industries and dealing with significant local opposition.

Despite initial political support, the ERC project faced significant hurdles. Congress demanded justification for the substantial investment, given that millions of dollars would be spent on construction and subsequent research activities. NASA successfully argued that no other location matched Boston's potential for the research center, emphasizing the anticipated nationwide benefits of farming out research projects to universities across the country.

Additionally, initial architectural plans, which included high towers and expansive complexes, exceeded the budget and required substantial revisions. These challenges led to ongoing debates within NASA and frequent design changes, causing delays and cost overruns.

Construction officially began in October 1966 under the supervision of the USACE. The foundational work for the high-rise program management building, low-rise laboratories, a personnel services building, a power plant and a warehouse got underway. By December 1967, significant progress had been made, and superstructures were nearing completion. The project was envisioned to be a sprawling complex that, upon completion, would employ 2,100 staff members, including scientists, engineers and technical workers.

Despite the progress, the ERC project faced an unexpected setback. On December 29, 1969, President Richard Nixon issued an executive order to terminate the ERC, effective June 30, 1970. This abrupt decision halted further construction, leaving only one twelve-story tower and five low-rise buildings completed. The closure was rumored to be a political move against the Kennedys and Massachusetts, which had not supported Nixon in the 1968 election.

The ERC's closure dealt a significant blow to Cambridge's redevelopment plans. Local officials, including those from MIT, protested the decision, highlighting the breach of contractual obligations and the anticipated economic impact. Efforts were made to prevent the site from being abandoned entirely.

John Volpe, who had recently been appointed secretary of transportation by Nixon and was a former Massachusetts governor, played a critical role in mitigating the impact of the ERC's closure. Volpe recognized the potential for the nearly completed facilities and advocated for their repurposing. Against the advice of some of his key advisors, Volpe facilitated the transfer of the ERC facilities to the Department of Transportation (DOT), which established the John A. Volpe National Transportation Systems Center on July 1, 1970. This move ensured that the buildings would be used for research and development in transportation systems, preserving some of the original vision for the site. Approximately 425 of the original 611 NASA staffers transitioned to the new center, maintaining continuity in the high-tech research workforce in the area.

PART III

★

KEY FIGURES AND EVENTS

PROFILES IN COLD WAR MASSACHUSETTS

Women's Contributions to Civil Defense and Military Preparedness

Women were supporting civil defense efforts in great numbers. Affiliated with the American Red Cross and other organizations, chapters of the Special Aid Society for American Preparedness Massachusetts Branch for Women began to spring up across the state with a mission to "encourage and promote patriotic education, sentiment and service among the people; and to aid in the establishment and maintenance of the National Defense." An article in March 1916 touted a presentation on the Special Aid Society, noting its purpose was to "give the women of this country an opportunity to organize in case of war or other disaster." Like other programs under the national Preparedness Movement, in addition to supporting effort in the war in Europe, the Special Aid Society worked locally to assist where needed. The Special Aid Society bylaws outline "training in the care of sickness," with classes in first aid and home nursing under the Red Cross and classes in making bandages and dressings through the Surgical Dressings Committee of the Women's Department of the National Civic Federation. Further, the Special Aid Society's skills included motor driving and repairing, telegraphy, signaling and wireless, cutting and sewing for hospital equipment and "organization for instant help in case of disaster of any kind," including "coordination of all agencies for relief and rehabilitation in providing shelter,

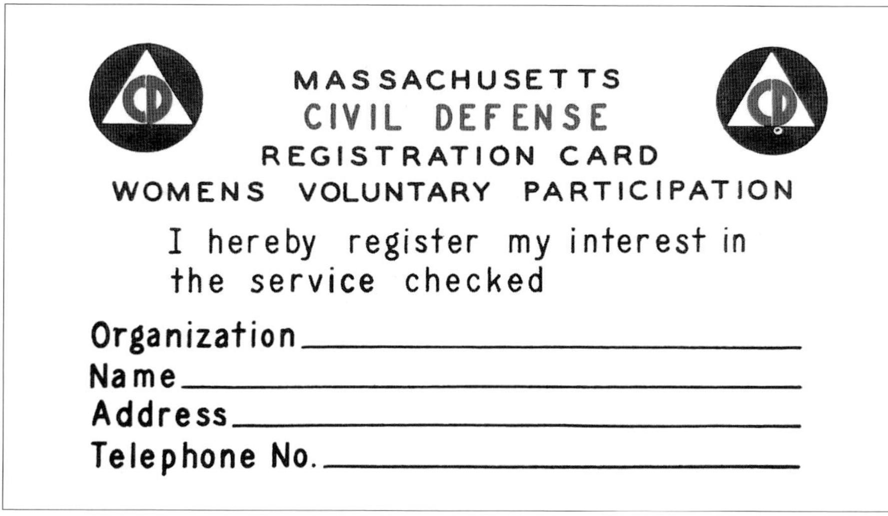

MASSACHUSETTS
CIVIL DEFENSE
REGISTRATION CARD
WOMENS VOLUNTARY PARTICIPATION

I hereby register my interest in
the service checked

Organization ______
Name ______
Address ______
Telephone No. ______

Women played a crucial role in Massachusetts civil defense activities, with the agency actively recruiting them for various key positions, emphasizing their vital contributions and responsibilities. *MEMA.*

food, clothing; uniting scattered families and in finding work." In February 1917, six hundred women attended a meeting of the Special Aid Society in Needham, where the president of the chapter, Mrs. Barrett Wendell, provided an update on the work of the group and it was announced that a headquarters was to be opened in the town hall.

By 1940, women were playing an increasing and more impactful role in preparedness and civil defense, including leadership roles. In February 1943, four hundred women from nine units of the Massachusetts Women's Defense Corps (MWDC) resigned en masse based on the corps' claim that their efforts had been undermined. They began a very public argument in the *Boston Globe* stating they believed "public safety cannot be served best" under the leadership of then-chair of the executive director of public safety, J. Wells Farley. MWDC Colonel Natalie Hays Hammond remarked on the way the units had been "hamstrung by the inexcusable failure of responsible officials to provide essential equipment," and in January 1943, she told the *Globe*, "The corps represented in fact a true democratic cross-section of the women of the state—all age groups, income levels, races and creeds had equal chance in the responsibility they were proud to share."

In September 1952, two British women capped off a five-day workshop in Sudbury hosted by the Massachusetts Civil Defense Agency, offering their collective experience on efforts during World War I in England.

Sara Woodward

Sara Foster Woodward was a prominent civil defense organizer and civic leader from Winchester. Born in 1910, she demonstrated early academic excellence, attending Mount Holyoke College at just sixteen years old and graduating in 1931.

In 1954, Woodward joined the Federal Civil Defense Administration (FCDA) and was appointed as the New England regional director of women's activities. She attended the Federal Civil Defense Training Center in Maryland, the predecessor to the Emergency Management Institute, in April that year. She worked tirelessly to engage women in civil defense efforts, collaborating with local organizations to create comprehensive programs.

Woodward was recognized for her careful oversight of a $10 million federal assistance grant aimed at repairing hurricane and flood damage in Massachusetts in 1954 and 1955. In 1955, Woodward traveled to Nevada to observe an atomic bomb test. During the test, she was stationed in a slit trench only two miles from the blast area.

Left: Mrs. Philip J. Woodward of Winchester, director of the Federal Civil Defense Administration Education Office for Region I, at a Mass Feeding Course, Fort Devens, 1953. *Digital Commonwealth.*

Opposite: Catherine Falvey of Somerville, a former Women's Army Corps major, was as an attorney and served as assistant director of the Federal Civil Defense Administration from 1951 to 1954. *National Archives.*

Woodward's dedication to civil defense continued as she took on a significant role in 1964, leading the Resources Contract Staff of the Massachusetts Civil Defense Agency. Her work focused on planning transportation and distribution routes for emergency supplies in case of disasters.

Her achievements in civil defense earned her commendations from President Lyndon B. Johnson and Massachusetts Governors John Volpe and Francis Sargent.

Catherine E. Falvey

Catherine E. Falvey (1910–1965) played a significant role in Massachusetts and broader national efforts, particularly in civil defense and women's involvement in these initiatives. Her career was marked by a blend of military service, legal work and political engagement, reflecting her dedication to public service and national security.

Falvey's political career began in 1938, when she served as a state representative from Somerville, Massachusetts, the youngest woman ever elected at the time, until 1940. Her early foray into politics set the stage for

her subsequent roles in public service. In 1942, she joined the first Women's Army Corps (WAC) contingent stationed in England, where she worked on General Dwight Eisenhower's staff during World War II, attaining the rank of major by the end of her service in 1946. Her military career included significant contributions to the Nuremberg Trials as part of the prosecuting team, showcasing her legal expertise and commitment to justice.

She was a graduate of Portia Law School and member of the Massachusetts and federal bars. In 1945, as a Massachusetts delegate to the Democratic Convention, she seconded the nomination for president of Harry S Truman. In 1946, Falvey made a bid for political office, campaigning in the Democratic primary for Massachusetts's Eleventh Congressional District, losing to John F. Kennedy.

Falvey's involvement in civil defense began in earnest in 1951, when she was appointed as the deputy administrator of Federal Civil Defense Agency in Natick. She also attended the Federal Civil Defense Training Center in Maryland in October 1959, the predecessor to the Emergency Management Institute.

John F. Kennedy (JFK): His Role in the Cold War

A secret bunker was constructed on Nantucket for President John F. Kennedy by the U.S. Navy Seabees. This bunker, designed to withstand nuclear blasts, was intended to protect the president and his family in the event of a nuclear attack while they were vacationing at the Kennedy family compound in Hyannis Port on Cape Cod. A similar bunker was built on Peanut Island near the Kennedy mansion in Palm Beach.

The Nantucket bunker, described as a Quonset hut buried under twelve feet of sand, lead and concrete, featured a semicircular rust-streaked portal emerging from a grassy hillock. The structure, assembled from sections of Quonset huts, included a tubular corrugated steel tunnel leading to a large half-cylinder interior. This design was based on bunkers that had withstood atomic tests in Nevada, ensuring it could provide effective shelter during a nuclear event. The bunker included a metal ladder leading to an escape hatch and was equipped with basic amenities for emergency survival.

Before the bunker was built, the site was part of a thirty-acre naval facility in the 1950s used to chart offshore conditions and detect enemy submarines. After its deactivation in 1976, the bunker fell into disrepair and was used as an office for the island's hunting club and a storage facility for county fairs.

Efforts are now underway to restore the bunker and possibly transform it into a museum. Local officials and community members are leading these efforts, aiming to revitalize the site and preserve this piece of Cold War history. The restoration proposal includes furnishing the bunker with period artifacts and opening it for public tours to educate future generations about this critical period in history.

However, the Nantucket bunker now faces a significant threat from coastal erosion. A coastal resilience study has identified it as being in a potential erosion zone, raising concerns about the long-term viability of investing in its preservation if the ocean could eventually claim it. Despite this threat, proponents of the restoration believe that preserving the bunker is crucial for maintaining a tangible link to the past.

NOTABLE EVENTS AND CASE STUDIES

Cuban Missile Crisis

On October 24, 1962, Massachusetts Governor Volpe held an emergency meeting with his department heads to enhance civil defense efforts in response to the escalating Cuban crisis. Volpe's office canceled all upcoming campaign activities to focus on preparedness. Similarly, Maine's governor, John H. Reed, met with his department heads, highlighting the seriousness of the situation, calling it the gravest crisis since World War II.

In Worcester, Mayor McGrath organized a high-level meeting to strategize emergency responses, driven by numerous anxious phone calls from residents. Measures were implemented, including designating schools as shelters, setting up a dedicated phone line for emergency information and instructing department heads to ensure readiness for any potential crisis.

Leicester's school department sponsored a drill involving students to familiarize them with emergency protocols. Hospitals across Massachusetts also prepared, with emergency plans and shelters ready to accommodate a surge in patients if needed.

Federal supplies started arriving in the state, providing shelters with medical, food and sanitary supplies. Cambridge's fire chief, Edmund Burke, noted ongoing preparations but no specific locations for shelters, with public buildings and schools being prepared as potential safe havens.

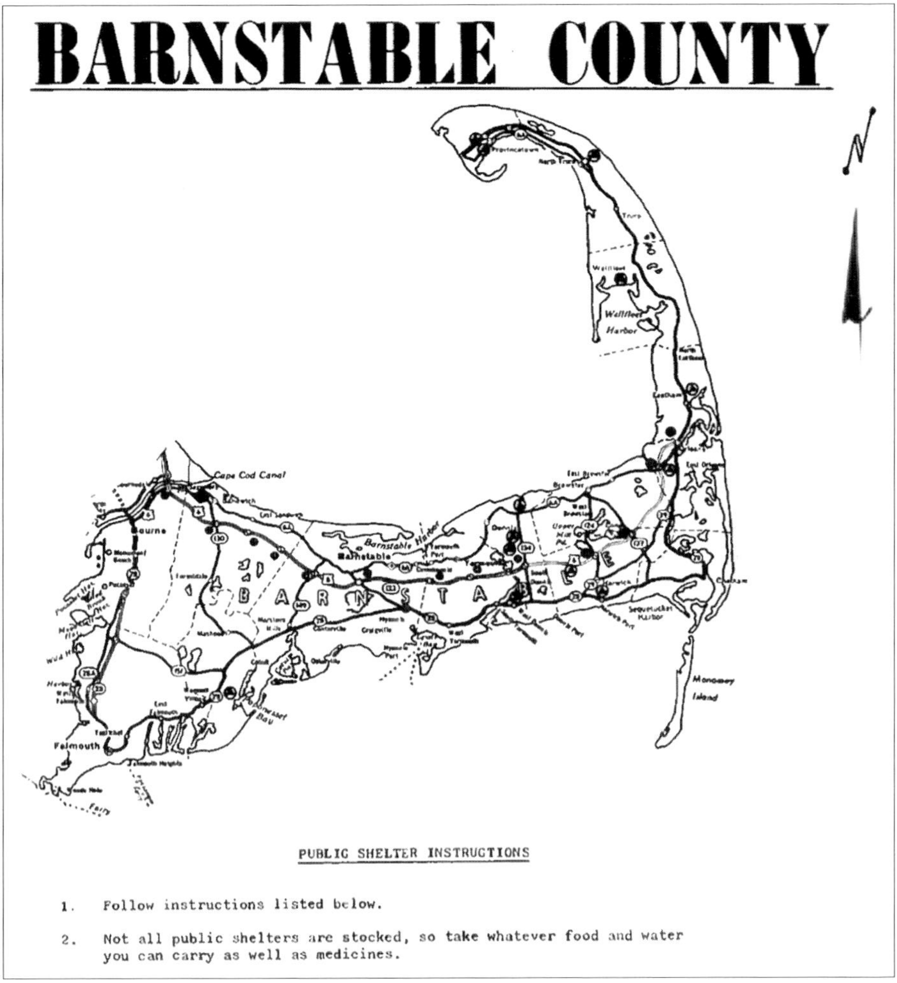

This Barnstable County map shows public shelter locations. Residents were advised to carry food, water and medicines because shelters might not be fully stocked. *FalloutFiveZero.*

New England civil defense authorities began to intensify programs for fallout protection due to international developments. The primary effort, particularly in Massachusetts, was to increase the licensing of shelters in schools, government buildings and commercial and industrial facilities that met minimum fallout protection standards.

At that time, 4,306 buildings in Massachusetts had been deemed suitable for fallout protection by federal agencies, but only 182 had been licensed. The state civil defense agency urged local directors to expedite the licensing of these buildings, already approved by the U.S. Army Corps of Engineers and the Navy Bureau of Yards and Docks. Additionally, the federal civil defense agency increased the stockpiling of supplies, including high-protein food and water, in government warehouses to ensure shelters were well equipped.

Licensed shelters were to have two weeks' worth of food and water supplies. Local officials faced challenges convincing private building owners to use their structures as public shelters.

Fallout Shelter Program

In the midst of the Cold War, anxieties surrounding nuclear war prompted a nationwide effort to identify and prepare fallout shelters. As of January 1, 1968, the national fallout shelter survey had identified 7,050 structures in Massachusetts capable of serving as public fallout shelters, offering a combined capacity of nearly three million spaces. These shelters were primarily concentrated in the state's larger cities. However, this left a substantial portion of the state's population, particularly those residing in smaller towns, rural areas, and suburbs, without adequate protection in the event of a nuclear attack.

Recognizing this critical vulnerability, both state and federal authorities sought measures to address the situation. Governor John A. Volpe announced a new initiative: the home fallout protection survey. This program, a product of investigations by the Department of Defense into expanding existing survey techniques to encompass smaller structures and private residences, aimed to assess the feasibility of utilizing private homes as fallout shelters.

To facilitate this survey, the Bureau of the Census initiated the process of mailing questionnaires to residents in 40 Massachusetts communities, including the city of Lynn. The questionnaires sought to gather information about the availability and characteristics of potential shelter spaces within private homes. In areas where mailing questionnaires was not feasible, the Bureau planned to employ enumerators to conduct in-person surveys and collect the necessary data.

The questionnaires were designed to be completed by householders within a week and returned promptly to ensure efficient data collection. To encourage participation, households that returned their questionnaires were promised a leaflet containing valuable information about enhancing the

In 1961, President Kennedy urged American families to build bomb shelters to protect themselves from potential atomic fallout, reflecting heightened national security concerns. *Springfield Morning Union.*

protective capabilities of their basements. The success of the survey hinged on robust public cooperation. It was emphasized that participating in the survey served the best interests of both individual householders and their families, as it could ultimately contribute to their safety and well-being in a potential nuclear emergency.

PART IV

★

POLITICS, MEDIA AND PUBLIC PERCEPTION

THE POLITICS OF COLD WAR MASSACHUSETTS

On March 11, 1955, the United States Senate's civil defense administrator advised a Senate Armed Services Subcommittee that all citizens should construct underground shelters immediately, equipped with enough food and water to last five to six days. This recommendation was based on understanding the potential effects of a hydrogen bomb, especially with the advancement of intercontinental guided missiles.

This testimony was a response to a complaint by Massachusetts Governor Christian A. Herter, who criticized the federal government for not providing adequate guidance to the states on protecting their populations from radiation fallout. Governor Herter expressed concerns about the lack of information on protective measures, such as whether raincoats were better than cloth coats or if riding in a closed automobile offered any protection. He emphasized that the states were unable to take even the most basic precautions and that swift decisions were needed at the federal level.

The concept of urban evacuation was put to the test on June 15, 1955, during Operation Alert, conducted by the Federal Civil Defense Administration in fifty-five cities across the United States. The simulated attacks began in Massachusetts, starting with New Bedford, followed by Providence and Boston.

The anticipated devastation was substantial. The Federal Civil Defense Administration estimated five million fatalities and nearly five million injuries in the event of an atomic bomb, with ten million people becoming homeless, creating significant welfare issues.

A Civil Defense Rescue Service vehicle stands by in Everett during Operation Alert in 1955, overseen by Boston's regional office. *Digital Commonwealth.*

The *New York Times* reported on the extensive impact of radioactive fallout, noting that vital centers of the nation would be paralyzed for weeks due to the hypothetical attacks.

Sentinel ABM at Sharpner's Pond (1969)

In November 1967, the Department of Defense announced that Boston would be the first of ten locations to receive a Sentinel Anti-Ballistic Missile (ABM) system. Throughout 1968, the U.S. Army Air Defense Command (ARADCOM), along with the Huntsville District and local U.S. Army Corps of Engineers Districts, evaluated possible sites around Boston. They eventually chose Camp Curtis Guild, a National Guard training base located in Reading, Lynnfield and Wakefield, for the nation's first ABM site. The Sharpner's Pond area in Harold Parker State Forest was selected for the missile launch site, while a radar site was planned for North Andover.

In September 1968, Brox Construction Company of Dracut, Massachusetts, was awarded the contract for the site access road, clearing and some excavation. Work began quickly after the corps gave notice to proceed on September 24. On January 22, 1969, Morrison-Knudsen Inc. of Boise, Idaho, was awarded a $2.2 million contract for preliminary construction work for Phase II of the project.

Public reaction to the project was initially subdued, but as the 1968 national election approached, Sentinel sites became a topic of debate. With construction already underway near Boston, opponents of Ballistic Missile Defense (BMD) had a tangible focal point for their protests.

On January 29, 1969, the corps hosted a public relations meeting at Reading High School to address resident concerns. Over one thousand people attended, including local and out-of-state BMD opponents, despite blizzard conditions. Army representatives faced boos and hostile arguments against the BMD system, and the meeting received wide publicity. An article published on February 2, 1969, in the *Boston Globe* featured former presidential aide Richard N. Goodwin, who argued that the Sentinel system would transfer the decision to use nuclear weapons from the president to local commanders. He also cited scientists from MIT, who had long contended that the Sentinel system would not protect the United States, Boston or nearby towns like Reading and Lynnfield.

In a letter to Secretary of Defense Melvin Laird, Senator Edward Kennedy called for a freeze on Sentinel construction, citing concerns about costs, threats to world peace and the danger of escalating the arms race. He pointed to the upcoming deliberations on the Nuclear Non-Proliferation Treaty as an opportunity for the Nixon administration to reconsider the Sentinel system.

Senator Kennedy's letter intensified the growing controversy in the Senate about the program. Consequently, Laird halted construction at Sharpner's Pond on February 4, pending a review of the Sentinel system. On March 14, President Nixon announced that a modified version of Sentinel, called Safeguard, would be deployed. As part of the Safeguard plan, the Sharpner's Pond site was abandoned, and the project at Camp Curtis Guild was discontinued.

CONCLUSION

Massachusetts played a pivotal role throughout the Cold War, embodying a multifaceted approach to national security and defense. The state's military bases were integral in housing missiles and maintaining advanced radar and communication systems, ensuring a robust defense network. These installations were vital in safeguarding the United States against potential threats during this tense period.

Civil defense efforts in Massachusetts showcased a well-coordinated response from federal, state and local authorities. Federal directives were effectively implemented at the state level, with local governments, especially in Boston and other cities, playing crucial roles in preparedness and protection. Public and private shelters were established, regular drills were conducted and comprehensive warning systems were deployed to keep the populace prepared for any eventuality.

Research institutions such as MIT and Lincoln Labs were at the forefront of technological advancements that bolstered national security. Their contributions in radar technology, energy and medical research not only enhanced defense capabilities but also drove innovation that had far-reaching impacts beyond the Cold War.

Massachusetts continues to support military initiatives, research and pioneering approaches in modern emergency management. The state remains a critical hub for defense activities, with ongoing military operations and advanced technology development. Research institutions still lead in cutting-edge projects, contributing to advancements in cybersecurity, space exploration and biomedical innovations.

Modern emergency management in Massachusetts is also noteworthy. The state leverages its historical experience and advanced technology to develop comprehensive strategies for disaster response and public safety. The emergency management headquarters, colloquially known as "the Bunker," remains central to coordinating these efforts, ensuring that Massachusetts is well prepared to handle contemporary challenges. In 2024, the Bunker was updated to enhance accessibility and address a broader range of functional needs for emergency management professionals, further reinforcing its role in supporting effective disaster response.

In summary, Massachusetts emerged as a cornerstone of the United States' Cold War strategy through its extensive military infrastructure, proactive civil defense measures and pioneering research efforts. Today, the state continues to play a vital role in national security and emergency management, underscoring its enduring importance in safeguarding the nation.

BIBLIOGRAPHY

Agency for Toxic Substances & Disease Registry. Public Health Assessment: Fort Devens–Sudbury Training Annex, 2010.

"Andover Nuclear Center Canceled by Conditions." *Boston Globe*, November 5, 1957, 3.

Argonne National Laboratory. Historic American Engineering Record: Cape Cod Air Station. 2000.

Arnold, David. "Blast from the Past." *Boston Sunday Globe Magazine*, March 14, 1999.

Atkinson, Leroy. "Western Massachusetts to Get Atomic Electric Power Sometime in 1960." *Springfield Sunday Republican*, November 24, 1957, 18.

"Atom Bombs 'Hit' in Area." *Springfield Republican*, April 29, 1961, 6.

"'Atoms for Peace' Show Coming to City in April." *Morning Union*, January 11, 1958, 20.

"Barnes to Be Connected to Military 'Hot Line.'" *Boston Globe*, March 23, 1966, 3.

Bartlett, K.S. "If You Want a Private Bomb Shelter Put It in the Cellar." *Boston Sunday Globe*, January 14, 1951.

"Bell System Nuclear Design Criteria." *Bell Labs Record*, January 1969.

Benzaquin, Paul. "Atoms for Peace for Youngsters at Children's Museum." *Boston Sunday Globe*, November 11, 1956, 84.

"Bill Requires 10-Mile Evacuation Zone Around All Nuclear Plants." *Daily Evening Item*, January 22, 1987, 3.

Bird, Grace. "Rebuilding Access to Former Nuke Site Could Cost $800K." *Athol Daily News*, February 6, 1987.

Bittelari, Lieutenant Colonel Thomas J. *Nike Missile History*. Massachusetts Army National Guard, n.d.

Black, Herbert. "Bay State Lacks Organization to Cope with Disaster If Disaster Hits Here—IV." *Boston Globe*, April 3, 1964, 17.

"Bomb Shelter Survey Planned for Springfield." *Boston Globe*, April 30, 1942, 3.
Booche, J. "Rowe a Pioneer of the Nuclear Age: Yankee Atomic Says Relationship with Town Strong." *Greenfield Recorder*, July 10, 1985, 21.
"Boston Common Garage to Be World's Biggest: 2 Underground Units to Hold 3000 Cars; Could Be Bomb Shelter." *Boston Globe*, November 17, 1961, 20.
"Boston 7th Atom Target Says Dever." *Boston Globe*, August 3, 1950, 1.
Bradley, Debra. "This Was a Test…but Not Everyone Knew about 'Nuclear Disaster.'" *Boston Globe*, March 20, 1981, 1.
Broncaccio, Diane. "Schools Grapple with Nuclear Emergency Plans." *Recorder*, July 1991.
Buchanan, David G., and John P. Johnson. "Natick Research and Development Laboratories." Historic American Engineering Record, National Park Service, Washington, D.C., 1984.
Burns, Frances. "Everybody Would Either Need Blood or Give It." *Boston Daily Globe*, October 11, 1950, 5.
———. "How a Hospital Will Keep Going." *Boston Sunday Globe*, October 8, 1950, 23.
———. "If Disaster or Bomb Hits City of Boston." *Boston Sunday Globe*, October 8, 1950, 5.
———. "More Will Die from Burns Than Radiation." *Boston Sunday Globe*, October 15, 1950.
———. "No Hysteria When Citizens Get Facts." *Boston Sunday Globe*, October 8, 1950, 12.
———. "350 'Refugees' Fed Emergency Rations in 12 Minutes." *Boston Daily Globe*, June 2, 1955, 19.
"Callahan to Offer Tunnels as Shelters." *Boston Globe*, December 6, 1961.
"Catherine E. Falvey, 54, Attorney, Ex-Legislator." *Boston Globe*, April 20, 1964, 37.
"CD Director." *Boston Globe*, May 18, 1976, 18.
"CD Is Stepping Up Licensing Shelters." *Springfield Transcript*, October 24, 1962.
Charles Stark Draper Laboratory. Draper, 2023.
"Civil Defense Agency Is Proposed for State." *Boston Evening Transcript*, June 20, 1950, 1.
"Civil Defense Buzzer System to Be Installed in Homes." *Berkshire Eagle*, November 11, 1961.
"Civil Defense Chief Is Named by President." *Boston Evening Transcript*, December 2, 1950.
"Civil Defense Cut 75% by Dukakis." *Boston Globe*, April 9, 1975, 2.
"Civil Defense Headquarters Moves to Natick." *Boston Globe*, August 12, 1951, 43.
"Civil Defense HQ Dedicated Nov. 16 in Framingham." *Boston Globe*, November 5, 1963, 4.
"Civil Defense Tests Home Buzz Alarm." *Boston Globe*, September 5, 1960.

"Civil Defense Test Successful as 'A Bomb' Falls." *Boston Globe*, August 15, 1951, 1.

"Civil Defense to Test Siren Coverage Today." *Boston Globe*, April 28, 1961.

"Civil Defense Work Speeded, Volpe Calls Parley Thursday." *Boston Globe*, October 24, 1962.

"Civil Defense Year Old." *Recorder*, July 20, 1951, 8.

"CONELRAD Obsolete: Wartime Radio Silence Due to Give Way to New Setup." *Boston Globe*, July 3, 1963, 2.

Curtis, William C., Jr. "Bay State Develops Relocation Plan for Nuclear Attack." *Boston Globe*, December 28, 1976, 3.

Cusano, Nicole. "Rowe Yankee Celebrates 30th Birthday." *Recorder*, November 1990.

Cutler, Samuel B. "Civil Defense Duties Assigned State Agencies." *Boston Globe*, September 15, 1950, 23.

———. "Dever Order Gives Towns, Cities OK on Civil Defense Plans." *Boston Globe*, October 19, 1950.

———. "156 Towns Fail to Heed Dever's Defense Edict." *Boston Globe*, September 26, 1950, 24.

———. "State Plans to Move Records; Boston Alerted for Attack." *Boston Globe*, December 19, 1950, 1.

Davis, Richie. "Emergency Plans in Place: CD Director: Towns Have All They Need." *Recorder*, June 1991.

"Defense Director Announces State Air Raid Signals." *Boston Globe*, December 17, 1950, 52.

Delaney, William P., and William W. Ward. "Radar Development at Lincoln Laboratory: An Overview of the First Fifty Years." *Lincoln Laboratory Journal* 12, no. 2 (2000): 147–66.

Del Papa, E. Michael, and Mary P. Warner. *A Historical Chronology of the Electronic Systems Division, 1947–1986*. 1987.

"Development of a Shelter Allocation and Use Plan for Boston." Stanford Research Institute, February 1963.

"Dever Orders Top Priority to Civilian Defense Planning." *Boston Globe*, September 21, 1950, 7.

"Dever Signs Bill Allotting $180,500 to Civil Defense." *Boston Globe*, March 9, 1951, 14.

"Dever to Reveal Target Areas to State's Mayors." *Boston Globe*, October 6, 1950, 17.

Doherty, Raymond. "Bay State CD Rushes 'Atom-Proof' Headquarters Under Ground at Framingham." *Boston Globe*, October 13, 1962.

Drew, Bernard A. "Operator, Give Me Long-Distance Lines." *Berkshire Eagle*, October 11, 2009.

Duffie, Warren, Jr. "A Revolutionary Relationship: The Navy and Woods Hole." *Future Force: Naval Science and Technology Magazine*, 2019.

"Efforts Are Paying Off: CD Is Making Progress Despite Apathy of Public." *Boston Globe*, December 19, 1960.

"Evacuating Hub Impossible Now, Says Maginnis." *Boston Daily Globe*, April 6, 1954, 7.

"Fallout Shelter Going Up in State House Lawn." *Worcester Telegram*, August 9, 1961, 14.

"Fallout Shelters Given More Stress by Governor." *Boston Globe*, September 19, 1961, 14.

"Fallout Shelters Not Catching On." *Springfield Transcript*, October 2, 1962.

"Fallout Shelter Survey Will Enter Second Phase." *Springfield Transcript*, June 21, 1962.

"Fighter Group Tied to 'Autovon' Circuit." *Boston Globe*, February 4, 1966, 3.

"First Revere Test Alert Starts at Dawn Today." *Boston Globe*, September 9, 1950, 1.

Fuller, Garrett. *History of AT&T Long Lines*. TelephoneWorld.org, 2018.

"Full Mobilization of Civilians Is Due Under New A-Bomb Defense Plan." *Springfield Morning Union*, December 7, 1949, 1.

Godsoe, William D. "Bill Would Demand School Fallout Shelters." *Boston Globe*, March 15, 1966, 2.

"Gov. Volpe Asks Fallout Shelter at Bowdoin Sq." *Boston Globe*, October 31, 1962.

"Hanscom Field, Bedford." *Boston Globe*, October 10, 1966, 2.

Harris, John. "Catherine E. Falvey Soon to Be Named to Top Defense Post." *Boston Globe*, October 27, 1951, 1.

Hayward, K.C., Jr. "Civil Defense Plan Calls Seabrook Evacuation Feasible." *Boston Sunday Globe*, December 16, 1984, 50.

Hirshson, Paul E. "Plan to Evacuate Cambridge in Nuclear Attack Criticized." *Boston Globe*, January 13, 1983, 22.

Historic American Engineering Record. Watertown Arsenal, Building No. 100 (Horace Hardy Lester Reactor). Wooley Avenue, Watertown, Middlesex County, Massachusetts. U.S. Custom House, Philadelphia: National Park Service, 1960.

"Home Bomb Shelters Not Popular in Suburbs." *Boston Globe*, December 19, 1960.

"Home Fallout Protection Survey Started." *North Adams Transcript*, February 7, 1966, 6.

"Hospitals Given Instructions for A-Attack Emergencies." *Boston Globe*, July 30, 1951, 24.

"Hub Garage, Bomb Shelter 'Interests' the President." *Berkshire County Eagle*, December 13, 1950, 44.

"Huge Radar Blimp Lands Here." *Boston Globe*, August 27, 1959.

"Hynes Sees Truman Today on Loan for Common Garage." *Boston Globe*, December 12, 1950, 7.

IBM. "Introduction to AN/FSQ-7 Combat Direction Central and AN/FSQ-8 Combat Control Central." January 1, 1959.

Jo, Angie. *Boston City Hall: Conception and Reception in the Era of Civil Defense*. 2014.

Joint Agreement Between Stony Brook Air Force Station (AMC) and Westover Air Force Base (SAC). 1954.

Katz, Tonnie. "Civil Defense—Empty: Few Are Concerned in Massachusetts." *Boston Globe*, March 14, 1976, 1.

Kelliher, Judith. "Health Board Hears AFSC Group on Anthrax Issue." *Daily Hampshire Gazette*, February 2, 1989.

———. "Health Board Hears Anthrax Debate." *Daily Hampshire Gazette*, April 27, 1989.

Ketter, Clarke. *3084th Aviation Depot Group Stony Brook Air Force Station: A History of a Cold War Mission*. N.d.

Kindleberger, R.S. "30 State Workers Cut by Dukakis Ordered Rehired." *Boston Globe*, November 25, 1975, 3.

Lahr, Ellen G. "Hancock Emergency Chief's 'Hobby' Provides Ultimate Security Shelter." *Berkshire Eagle*, September 5, 1999.

Larrabee, Donald R. "Truman Helped Goldfine on Boston CD Shelter Plan." *Transcript-Telegram*, June 30, 1958.

"Legionnaires to Man 216 Air Raid Posts in 'Operation Lookout.'" *Boston Globe*, June 18, 1949.

Lewis, William J. "Hub Firm Gets 1st Contract: $93 Million Shelter Survey to Start Immediately in N.E." *Boston Globe*, December 6, 1961.

Lincoln, Gould. "Rep. Kennedy 'Shocked' by Civil Defense Setup." *Boston Globe*, October 10, 1949.

Long Lines Department—Plant Division One. *The Latest Word in Communications*. New York, 1947.

Lonnquest, John C., and David F. Winkler. *To Defend and Deter: The Legacy of the U.S. Cold War Missile Program*. 1996.

"Loyalty Oaths for All Connected with Civil Defense." *Boston Globe*, May 16, 1951, 2.

Lyons, Louis M. "Bomb Shelters for Boston." *Boston Globe*, July 29, 1942, 1.

"Markey Criticizes Seabrook Move." *Boston Globe*, October 28, 1986, 23.

"Mass. Civil Defense—'Operation Hampden Alert.'" *Springfield Sunday Republican*, April 17, 1966, 25A.

Massachusetts Emergency Management Agency (MEMA). Headquarters, "The Bunker."

Matesky, Edwin. "Tunnel 'Shelter' for 31,300; Only One More for 50 or More." *North Adams Transcript*, October 26, 1962.

"Mayor, Sloan to Submit City's CD Plans to State Agency." *Springfield Morning Union*, August 9, 1950, 13.

McCarthy, Frederick D. "Andover to Get Huge A-Center Worth $5 Million." *Boston Globe*, December 10, 1956, 1.

———. "3rd N.E. Atom Plant Is Set for Andover." *Boston Globe*, December 11, 1956, 3.

McLean, Robert A. "4306 Fallout Shelters in State—But Most Are Unmarked, Unstocked." *Boston Globe*, October 28, 1962.

———. "Local CD Picture Fuzzy; State Awaits U.S. Action." *Boston Globe*, December 13, 1961.

———. "State Civil Defense Gets Most Intensive Test Friday." *Boston Sunday Globe*, April 12, 1959.

Memories of Experiences on Stony Brook Air Force Station: An Operational Storage Site of the United States Air Force 1954–1971. N.d.

MIT Lincoln Laboratory. *SAGE: Semi-Automatic Ground Environment Air Defense System*. N.d.

"M.I.T.'s Bunker to Set Up State A-Bomb Defense." *Boston Globe*, September 9, 1950, 1.

"M.I.T.'s Killian Heads Atom Peace Awards." *Berkshire County Eagle*, September 27, 1955, 13.

"Mock Air Raid Set Here Tuesday in Giant U.S. Civil Defense Test." *Boston Globe*, May 1, 1960.

Mohl, Bruce. "Professor Agrees to Advise Dukakis on Seabrook After Chernobyl Study." *Boston Globe*, May 29, 1986, 1.

Monteyne, David Patrick. *Shelter from the Elements: Architecture and Civil Defense During the Early Cold War*. 2005.

Moulton, Stanley. "Coal Plant: A Possibility for Montague." *Springfield Union*, April 2, 1979, 1.

Nadolski, Richard. "Underground Defense Workers Coming Up for Good." *Sunday Republican*, December 17, 1989, B22.

Naval Facilities Engineering Command. *Helping to Win the Cold War: A History of NWIIRP Bedford*. U.S. Navy, 2019.

"Needham Heads New Group of CD Advisors." *Boston Daily Globe*, March 26, 1954, 13.

"N.E. Military Stand Ready; Civil Defense Plans Pressed." *Berkshire Eagle*, October 24, 1962.

"New York–Boston Radio Relay Inaugurated." *Telephone News*, 1948.

"NRC Denies Seabrook Test License." *Daily Evening Item*, January 23, 1987, 3.

Nyhan, David, and Stephen A. Kurkjian. "New Light Thrown on 1974 Bomb Hoax: FBI Helped Hub Investigate Nuclear Ransom Threat." *Boston Sunday Globe*, November 29, 1981, A17.

O'Donnell, Richard W. "$1.3 Million Structure: Maynard Hill to House CD Center." *Boston Sunday Globe*, May 1, 1966, 27.

Parkman, Aubrey. *Army Engineers in New England (1775–1975)*. USACE, 1978.

Pfarrer, Steve. "UM Ends Anthrax Research." *Daily Hampshire Gazette*, December 19, 1997, 9.

Pioneer Valley Planning Commission. *An Historical Walking Tour of Westover Air Reserve Base*. 1993.

"Plant to Tell 30,570 of Emergency Plan." *Boston Globe*, May 23, 1980, 2.

Pokorny, Brad. "Amesbury to Consider Not Cooperating on Evacuation Planning." *Boston Globe*, November 16, 1985, 23.

———. "Seabrook's Builders May Seek 2-Mile Zone." *Boston Globe*, September 27, 1986, 1, 19.

"Police and Civil Defense Agencies Act Fast Here." *Springfield Daily News*, December 8, 1941, 1.

"Power Plant Enemy May Make Legal History." *Boston Globe*, April 1, 1974, 21.

Raytheon Company. *100 Years of Era-Defining Innovation*. 2022.

Robinson, Roderick. "UMass Conducts Germ Warfare." *Daily Hampshire Gazette*, November 14, 1988.

Roche, B.J. "Antinuclear Efforts Refocused: Rowe Yankee Plant Foes Seek to Revise Evacuation Plan." *Boston Globe*, September 16, 1991.

Rolbein, Seth. "City Limits: Boston's Ring of Fire." *Boston Magazine*, February 1995.

Rose, Jim. "Bunker N9 and Nuclear ASROC." *Friends of Wompatuck State Park Newsletter*, Winter 2007, 1–2.

"Rowe Atomic Plant to Be No Eye-Sore: Hopeful Townsfolk Expect Plant to Be Employment Boon." *Boston Daily Globe*, February 10, 1956, 1.

"Rule May Give Seabrook License Despite Dukakis." *Athol Daily News*, February 6, 1987, 10.

"Sara Woodward, 75: Honored for Civil Defense Work." *Boston Globe*, May 20, 1988, 65.

Sege, Irene. "If N-War Threatens, 'Hubbub' Is Ready." *Boston Globe*, June 9, 1982, 1.

Shimabukuo, Tom M. "The Next Generation CONUS AUTOVON." *IEEE Transactions on Communications*, September 1980.

Special Collections and University Archives. *Montague Nuclear Power Station Environmental Report*. University Libraries, UMass–Amherst, 1975.

"State Health Head Tells Washington of Blood-Typing Plan." *Boston Globe*, March 6, 1951, 28.

Stewart, Jay. "No Need to Fear Radioactivity Long After Bomb Blast." *Boston Globe*, August 13, 1950, 1.

Sullivan, Elizabeth. "Conelrad Test Uneven, Noisy, Hard to Understand." *Boston Sunday Globe*, July 21, 1956.

Talusan, Grace. "Did You Hear the One About MIT's Little Nuclear Reactor?" *Boston Magazine*, August 2011.

Taylor, Holly A. "Hancock CD Director's Shelter Has Defense Against Attackers." *Berkshire Eagle*, August 19, 1980, 3.

Thompson, Richard, and Frank Bogardus. "President Speaks to 5000 at Amherst: Plane Late at Westover for Frost Rites at College." *North Adams Transcript*, October 26, 1963.

Thornton, Mary. "Missiles Airlifted over Weymouth." *Boston Globe*, May 22, 1974.

"To Build Atomic Fall-Out Shelter in Wilbraham." *Transcript*, October 28, 1958.

"25,000 'Spotters' in Air Warning Tests Tomorrow." *Boston Globe*, September 9, 1949.

Tye, Larry. "Seabrook Eyes Fort Devens for Accident Evacuation." *Boston Globe*, September 18, 1987.

U.S. Air Combat Command. *Historical and Architectural Documentation Reports of North Truro Air Force Station*. 1995.

U.S. Atomic Energy Commission. *Tenth Annual Report of the Oak Ridge Institute of Nuclear Studies*. 1956.

"U.S. Civil Defense Agency Advocated by Mayors' Group." *Boston Globe*, February 2, 1942, 3.

U.S. Navy. *Helping to Win the Cold War: A History of NWIIRP Bedford*. 2019.

"Volpe Sees Long Crisis: Governor Urges Families Act on Shelters." *Boston Globe*, October 26, 1962.

Warsh, David. "Reaping Benefits of the Whirlwind." *Boston Globe*, June 9, 1985, 79, 90.

"Winchester Woman One of 75 Taking Part in A-Bomb Test." *Boston Daily Globe*, April 27, 1955, 9.

Winkler, David F., and Julie L. Webster. *Searching the Skies: The Legacy of the United States Cold War Defense Radar Program*. 1997.

Wysocki, Ronald. "Civil Defense Force Outnumbers All Police: Bay State's Uniformed Trained Auxiliary Has 11,000 Men." *Boston Globe*, July 24, 1960.

———. "Gigantic Shelter Under Boston Common: Room for 22,000 Persons If A-Blast Should Hit." *Boston Globe*, May 30, 1960.

ABOUT THE AUTHOR

Joshua Shanley has dedicated over thirty-two years to public safety, including his service as a firefighter-paramedic in New York and Massachusetts. He also served as a canine handler for FEMA Urban Search and Rescue Task Force, Massachusetts Task Force 1. Joshua currently works with the Massachusetts Emergency Management Agency and the Massachusetts Department of Fire Services. He participated in the efforts at the World Trade Center in both 1993 and 2001. He has taught at Purdue Global University, School of Public Safety for nearly twenty years. He is the author of several books on local history, including *Northampton Fires and Firefighting* and *The Connecticut River Valley Flood of 1936*.

For more photos, stories, links to sources or with any questions, please visit: www.ColdWarMass.org